D1598681

Laura

Laura

A Case for the Modularity of Language

Jeni E. Yamada

A Bradford Book
The MIT Press
Cambridge, Massachusetts
London, England

362.3
419L

© 1990 Massachusetts Institute of Technology

All rights reserved. No part of this book may be reproduced in any form by any electronic or mechanical means (including photocopying, recording, or information storage and retrieval) without permission in writing from the publisher.

This book was set in Palatino by Compset, Inc.
and printed and bound by Halliday Lithographs in the United States of America.

Library of Congress Cataloging-in-Publication Data

Yamada, Jeni Ellen, 1951—
    Laura : a case for the modularity of language / Jeni E. Yamada.
       p.   cm. — (Issues in the biology of language and cognition)
    "A Bradford book."
    ISBN 0-262-24030-0
    1. Mentally handicapped—Language—Case studies.   I.   Title.
    II. Series.
RC570.7.Y35   1990
362.1'9685889—dc20   90-39106
        M3   CIP

Contents

UNIVERSITY LIBRARIES
CARNEGIE MELLON UNIVERSITY
PITTSBURGH, PA   15213-3890

Foreword

As with any other common locution, the expression 'knowing a language' will not *usually* occasion any problem. If I claim to know French, you may reasonably assume that I could hold a moderately sensible conversation with a monolingual speaker of that language. Nonetheless, there is a hidden *ceteris paribus* clause: I could be mentally retarded, in the which case you might not be very impressed by the content of my remarks; alternatively I might pursue my own brilliant line of thought in blithe disregard of the conversational demands of your utterances. There are, in short, a number of ways in which my communication in French may fail other than frightful phonology, a tendency to put the adjective in front of the noun, and total inability to recall the correct inflectional forms of irregular verbs.

We may distinguish, then, with Chomsky (1980), three broad domains of knowledge of language, three "interacting but distinct components" of language and language use. In the first place, there is the grammatical competence characterized by "the rules that form syntactic constructions or phonological or semantic patterns of varied sorts." Second, there is "the system of object-reference and also such relations as 'agent,' 'goal,' 'instrument,' and the like"—"a 'conceptual' system" in one sense of that highly ambiguous word (Chomsky, 1980). Third, we may distinguish "pragmatic competence," a system that underlies the ability to use grammatical and conceptual knowledge "to achieve certain ends and purposes" (Chomsky, 1980).

If these distinctions carve cognition into even approximately correct biological domains, we might expect that (relatively) focal brain damage acquired in adult life could selectively impair one competence while leaving the others (relatively) intact.

And, to a first approximation, this is indeed what we find. Many aphasic patients with grossly abnormal grammatical abilities show little generalized conceptual loss. There is, as Zangwill (1969) writes, "no clear relation between severity of language disorder and severity of intellectual loss." In cases where the syntactic encoding (and decoding) of 'agent', 'goal' and 'instrument' etc. as thematic roles *within* the linguistic system is profoundly impaired (Caplan and Hildebrandt, 1988), there is no convincing evidence for dissolution of the basic conceptual relations themselves. Similarly, within the limits imposed by a restricted or disordered grammatical system, such patients may use whatever speech remains to them in a pragmatically coherent fashion. Appropriate affect, with good insight into the linguistic deficit, is not uncommon in the nonfluent aphasias. The patient may deploy his fractured native language as well as I deploy my fractured (non-native) French; communicative effectiveness with respect to ends and purposes is not coextensive with grammatical correctness in either case.

By contrast, selective disorder of object-reference and knowledge can be seen in a variety of patients with otherwise fairly intact syntactic abilities as assessed by both expression and comprehension. Warrington (1975) reported patients with diffuse cerebral lesions but little or no aphasia other than an impoverished vocabulary. The patients showed impaired knowledge of concrete objects and their names that could not be accounted for by intellectual deterioration, sensory or perceptual deficits, or 'expressive' aphasia *per se*. A very extensive literature is now available on such cases of 'semantic memory' impairment (Riddoch et al., 1988), after closed head injury (Farah et al., 1989), herpes encephalitis (Sartori and Job, 1988), and dementia of the Alzheimer type (Chertkow and Bub, 1990). Exactly how the category-specificity seen in such cases should be characterized and explained is an open question (Shallice, 1988; McCarthy and Warrington, 1988; Marshall, 1988; Damasio, 1989). But it is not at issue that these lexico-conceptual deficits can dissociate from disorders of grammatical processing.

There is also evidence for the selective impairment of pragmatic aspects of language. Such deficits appear to be most common and extensive in patients with right hemisphere damage who would not be characterized as 'aphasic' by any traditional criteria. The range of impairments observed is something of a mixed bag; 'pragmatic' in this literature is an adjective frequently applied when the disorder has no clear position within any better understood component of the language faculty. Nonetheless, it does seem that problems with the expression and comprehension of idioms, of such rhetorical devices as irony, sarcasm (and other types of 'humor'), of indirect commands and requests, of linguistic inferencing, and of 'nonliteral' language in general is selectively impaired by right hemisphere lesion (Kaplan et al., 1990). Failure to compute 'relevance' criteria (Sperber and Wilson, 1986) or understand meaningful violations of Gricean conversational maxims (Grice, 1978) would appear to be implicated. Whatever the ultimate status of current data in this area, it is, again, not in dispute that an inability to appreciate the pragmatic force of utterances can be dissociated from both conceptual ('semantic') and grammatical ('syntactic') deficits *per se.*

The evidence, then, from acquired lesions in adult life is (broadly) consistent with Chomsky's partitioning of language knowledge and use into three "interacting but distinct components" (Chomsky, 1980), grammatical, conceptual, and pragmatic.

It thus becomes plausible to inquire whether a similar fractionation is found in developmental disorders. Are the genetic, epigenetic, and maturational constraints upon the growth of the language faculty such that selective disorder of one of these components can be observed?

Cases of developmental dissociation between language as syntactic structure, as lexico-conceptual system, and as pragmatic instrument are well-known. Some of the best studied examples have been children where a rich cognitive system can only be expressed by a very limited range of grammatical devices. The investigations of Genie, a child isolated for many years from linguistic input and normal human contact, reported by Curtiss (1977) are a case in point. Once exposed to a normal (indeed supernormal) environment at the age of 13, Genie rapidly displayed an ability to represent (and talk about) the world (past, present, and future; animate and inanimate; physical and mental; actual and conditional) in a humanly appropriate fashion. But her capacity to express her cognitive representations in language remained severely impaired. Vocabulary acquisition progressed well, but her speech had little grammatical structure beyond linear juxtaposition of major lexical items. The hierarchical organization of syntactic representation was conspicuously lacking (Curtiss, 1981). Similarly, in cases of 'developmental dysphasia' that may have a genetic basis (Hurst et al., 1990) there is no reason to believe that the grammatical impairment is secondary to conceptual deficit (Gopnik, 1990).

By contrast, children have been described with gross cognitive deficits who nonetheless manifest a strikingly intact ability to acquire language *qua* formal grammatical system. The phenomenon can be seen in some hydrocephalic children, in Williams syndrome, and in Turner and Noonan syndrome (Curtiss, 1988). Even the ability to develop normal reading and writing skills (as transcoding procedures) is found in the context of severe mental deficiency but syntactically well-developed language (Cossu and Marshall, 1990). Antony, described by Curtiss and Yamada (1981), had an IQ in the 50s yet used x Foreword

a syntactically rich language, including movement, complementation, and embedding. He could appropriately mark lexical items for syntactic class, subcategorization, and case, but made frequent errors in semantic feature specification. Failure to appreciate presupposition and implicatives further compounded Antony's difficulties with communication in language. John, reported by Blank, Gessner, and Esposito (1978), showed excellent language functioning in that he produced an age-appropriate range of syntactically and semantically well-formed expressions. But he was almost totally unable to use that system in interpersonal communication; his attempts to initiate conversation were pragmatically bizarre, and his responses to questions had little relationship to the content thereof.

Laura: A Case for the Modularity of Language is a significant addition to the literature on developmental psycholinguistics in which these issues are discussed. Jeni Yamada has provided us with a detailed single-class study of a teenager with an IQ in the 40s who has nevertheless acquired phonological, morphological, and syntactic skills at a very high level. In some domains, there is impairment at the conceptual level with respect to time, manner, dimensionality, and number, and this is reflected in word choices that are semantically inappropriate. Pragmatic deficits are also observed—relevance and informativeness criteria fail to be met and discourse topics cannot be maintained. Extensive testing of nonlanguage skill and cognition reveals very profound retardation, and Piagetian tasks in particular occasion almost complete failure. Yet, despite this background of (almost) global impairment, language *qua* formal system of rules and representations has emerged intact.

As Yamada argues, such data refute attempts to 'reduce' the ontogenetic growth of the linguistic system to the cognitive, social, and perceptual factors that undoubtedly interact with language acquisition and use, in the broader sense of 'language' (Piatelli-Palmarini, 1980). Jeni Yamada's monograph stands both as an important contribution in its own right and will also inspire others to study theoretically revealing cases of developmental disorder in the same detail that is now *de rigueur* in the investigation of acquired pathology.

John C. Marshall

References

Blank, M., Gessner, M., and Esposito, A., 1978. Language without communication: A case study. *Journal of Child Language*, 6, 329–352.
Caplan, D. and Hildebrandt, N., 1988. *Disorders of Syntactic Comprehension*. Cambridge, Mass.: The MIT Press

Chertkow, H. and Bub, D., 1990. Semantic memory loss in dementia of the Alzheimer's type. In: *Modular Deficits in Alzheimer's Disease* (M. F. Schwartz, ed.). Cambridge, Mass.: The MIT Press.

Chomsky, N., 1980. *Rules and Representations*. New York: Columbia University Press.

Cossu, G. and Marshall, J. C., 1990. Are cognitive skills a prerequisite for learning to read and write? *Cognitive Neuropsychology, 7*, 21–40.

Curtiss, S., 1977. *Genie: A Psycholinguistic study of a modern-day 'Wild Child'*. New York: Academic Press.

Curtiss, S., 1981. Dissociations between language and cognition. *Journal of Autism and Developmental Disorders, 11*, 15–30.

Curtiss, S., 1988. The special talent of grammar acquisition. In: *The Exceptional Brain* (L. K. Obler and D. Fein, eds.). New York: The Guildford Press.

Curtiss, S. and Yamada, J., 1981. Selectively intact grammatical development in a retarded child. *UCLA Working Papers in Cognitive Linguistics, 3*, 61–91.

Damasio, A. R., 1989. Time-locked multiregional retroactivation: A systems-level proposal for the neural substrates of recall and recognition. *Cognition, 33*, 25–62.

Farah, M. J., Hammond, K. M., Mehta, Z., and Ratcliff, G., 1989. Category-specificity and modality-specificity in semantic memory. *Neuropsychologia, 27*, 193–200.

Gopnik, M., 1990. Feature-blind grammar and dysphasia. *Nature, 344*, 715.

Grice, P., 1978. Further notes on logic and conversation. In *Syntax and Semantics: Volume 3, Speech Acts* (P. Cole, ed.). New York: Academic Press.

Hurst, J. A., Baraitser, M., Anger, E., Graham, F., and Norell, S., 1990. An extended family with a dominantly inherited speech disorder. *Developmental Medicine and Child Neurology, 32*, 352–355.

Kaplan, J. A., Brownell, H. H., Jacobs, J. R., and Gardner, H., 1990. The effects of right hemisphere damage on the pragmatic interpretation of conversational remarks. *Brain and Language, 38*, 315–333.

Marshall, J. C., 1988. Sensation and semantics. *Nature, 334*, 378.

McCarthy, R. A., and Warrington, E. K., 1988. Evidence for modality specific meaning systems in the brain. *Nature, 334*, 428–430.

Piatelli-Palmarini, M., eds., 1980. *Language and Learning: The Debate between Jean Piaget and Noam Chomsky*. Cambridge, Mass.: Harvard University Press.

Riddoch, M. J., Humphreys, G. W., Coltheart, M., and Funnell, E., 1988. Semantic systems or system? Neuropsychological evidence reexamined. *Cognitive Neuropsychology, 5*, 3–25.

Sartori, G., and Job, R., 1988. The oyster with four legs: A neuropsychological study of the interaction of visual and semantic information. *Cognitive Neuropsychology, 5*, 105–132.

Shallice, T., 1988. Specialization within the semantic system. *Cognitive Neuropsychology, 5*, 133–142.

Sperber, D., and Wilson D., 1986. *Relevance*. Cambridge, Mass.: Harvard University Press.

Warrington, E. K., 1975. The selective impairment of semantic memory. *Quarterly Journal of Experimental Psychology, 27*, 635–657.

Zangwill, O. L., 1969. Intellectual status in aphasia. In *Disorders of Speech Perception, and Symbolic Behaviour* P. J. Vinken and G. W. Bruyn, eds. Amsterdam: North-Holland.

Acknowledgments

So many people have contributed to this project in significant ways. I want to thank Vicki Fromkin and John Marshall, who believed enough in the value of this study to insist that this book be finished. Both provided crucial comments, suggestions, and encouragement. I also owe a great deal to Susie Curtiss whose insights and input have always been invaluable. We collaborated on much of the initial testing of Laura. Many thanks, too, to Eran Zaidel for originally referring this case to us and for key comments on the data and discussion presented here. Pam Munro, Paul Schachter, and Evelyn Hatch made helpful suggestions. I am also grateful for discussion with Dan Kempler, Diana Van Lancker, Jennifer Buchwald, Judy Reilly, and Peter Tanguay, on various relevant topics. For helping with all the little (but important) things that needed to be done during the study, acknowledgments go to Cathy Jackson, Jan Scott, Delores Crawford, and Mark Abelson. Thanks, too, to Sandy Ferrari Disner, for some last-minute advice.

I also feel a deep gratitude to Laura's parents, who were always so supportive and involved. Throughout the study they offered crucial information regarding Laura's background and abilities and were often able to shed light on their daughter's more mystifying utterances. Laura's father always asked pertinent questions and her mother shared her wonderful "archives." Numerous selections appear here and capture Laura as an infant and young child. Laura's various teachers, speech therapists, and caretakers were wonderfully cooperative, contributing useful information regarding Laura's behavior and functioning.

My mother Mitsu, mother-in-law Edith, and father Yosh took time out of their busy professional lives to help with child care during the data collection and writing phases of this project. Special thanks go to my husband Phil, for his computer wizardry, his eye for detail and aesthetics, and his constant support. A microbiologist by day and a brilliant editor and "research assistant" by night, he got me through numerous high-tech perils and helped me navigate the text through to the finishing stages. My sons Aaron, Jason, and Adam provided many enjoyable albeit maddening distractions as well as some very memorable quotes.

Thanks, too, to Harry Stanton, Joanna Poole, and all the folks at MIT Press/Bradford Books for being so supportive and patient and to Anne Mark for her terrific, fine-grained copyediting.

Ultimate thanks, of course, must go to Laura, for simply being herself.

Prologue

Laura, previously known by her case name "Marta," first came to the attention of researchers as a result of her parents' astute observation that there was something very unusual about their fourth daughter. Laura's father, a well-known historian, happened to attend a lecture at a nearby university on language and the brain. During the talk the speaker gave examples of jargon aphasic speech, in which individuals produce complex, nonsensical utterances without apparent understanding of what they are saying. According to Laura's father, the examples sounded uncannily like his retarded daughter's utterances. Laura had not suffered any known postnatal traumatic insult but rather had shown unusual characteristics in her language throughout her development. Might there be something remarkable about her brain organization? Laura's father wondered whether a study of Laura would be of interest to researchers and in turn hoped that elucidation of her abilities might lead to more effective educational approaches for her.

He called Eran Zaidel, who was doing split-brain research at Caltech at the time. Dr. Zaidel in turn contacted Susan Curtiss at UCLA, thinking that her group, of which I was a member, might be intrigued by the case. Dr. Curtiss is well known for her language study of "Genie," a young girl who was deprived of linguistic, social, and emotional stimulation during crucial developmental years (Curtiss 1977).

The case sounded provocative. We made immediate arrangements to meet Laura and her parents. It was fall of 1979.

Over the next several years I developed a special relationship with Laura, documenting her unusual profile through study of her linguistic and nonlinguistic abilities.

This book is gratefully dedicated to Laura, to Laura's mother who nurtured and raised her, and to the memory of Laura's father, whose insight helped bring this case to light.

Laura

Chapter 1
Introduction

Child: (thoughtfully) I not man, Mommy,
Mother: You're not a man?
Child: I boy.
Mother: Yes, you're a boy.
Child: I child.
Dialogue with Aaron, 24 ½ months

1.1 Background

Human beings are not content simply to exist. We feel compelled to ponder and philosophize. And not only do we think, we think about thinking, and even think about thinking about thinking.

> Rivers flow
> The sea sings
> Oceans roar
> Tides rise
> Who am I?
> A small pebble
> On a giant shore;
> Who am I
> To ask who I am?
> Isn't it enough to be?
>   American Indian (cited in Mason 1977)

Philosophical questions such as "Who am I?" and "What is man?" are archetypal, appearing often in the works of scholars and philosophers. In contrast to many other early philosophers who were more concerned with the external physical world, Socrates recognized that there is no uncharted territory so complex and captivating as the human mind. Aristotle, curious about the origins of knowledge, wondered about innateness. Are we born knowing what we know of the world or must everything be acquired from experience?

During the seventeenth and eighteenth centuries Descartes, Locke, Leibnitz, Berkeley, Hume, and Kant grappled with questions related to man and mind. Today questions about the nature of human knowledge still captivate us. Cognitive science has blossomed into a serious field of inquiry benefiting from advances in such areas as neurology and medicine as well as psychology, linguistics, and education (for example see discussion in Gardner 1985).

One key question involves what may be the most complex human cognitive capacity. What is language? We have yet to agree upon what constitutes the appropriate domain of study in resolving this question. Should the boundaries of inquiry be closely or widely drawn? Is language an independent, unique cognitive system, involving task-specific or faculty-specific mechanisms? Or can it be wholly accounted for by general nonlinguistic cognitive, perceptual, and social factors? These questions reflect two schools of thought: the former, narrower point of view that to understand language we must consider specifically linguistic issues versus the latter, broader point of view that to elucidate language principles we must necessarily consider both linguistic and nonlinguistic factors.

One vital issue is the relationship between language and cognition. Elucidation of the relationship between language and other mental functions may be crucial to our understanding of the cognitive principles underlying language.

An approach that has enjoyed widespread support during the twentieth century has been a belief in the primacy of cognition. According to Piaget (1926, 1951, 1954, 1980) and his followers, language is simply part of a more general cognitive capacity, emerging out of sensorimotor intelligence and comprising but one expression of the semiotic function (Sinclair 1975b; Bates et al. 1977; Bates 1979). The view that cognition is a general human capacity upon which language rests has been called the *Cognitive Hypothesis* (Cromer 1974b, 1976a, 1981). The strong form of this hypothesis holds that cognitive attainments are both necessary and sufficient for language acquisition. This version of the theory has fallen out of favor due to mounting empirical counterevidence. The more popular weak form holds that although cognitive abilities may not be sufficient, they are at least necessary for language learning.

In view of new data, some do not believe that general cognitive stages or levels are necessarily associated with language, believing instead that specific cognitive attainments are prerequisite to specific linguistic attainments (see, for example, Ferreiro 1971). Gopnick and Meltzhoff (1986) have spoken of the "specificity hypothesis."

Another related view, the *Correlational Hypothesis*, holds that manifestations of abilities across domains are reflections of a third, shared underlying governing mechanism. It is this general underlying mechanism or set of principles governing language and other forms of cognition that is seen as prerequisite to language (Cromer 1974b, 1976a; Bates et al. 1977; Bates 1979; Miller 1981; Piatelli-Palmarini 1980). The abilities to classify, categorize, extract or abduce rules, and construct hierarchical relationships, for example, may be general abilities that manifest themselves in various cognitive domains, including language (Maratsos and Chalkley 1980; Piaget and Inhelder 1959; Sinclair (de Zwart) 1971, 1973; Greenfield, Nelson, and Saltzman 1972; Goodson and Greenfield 1975). Maratsos and Chalkley (1980) describe language learning as an expression of a general human inductive capacity that enables the individual to make generalizations from the distributional properties of grammatical classes and categories.

At the other end of the theoretical spectrum are those who argue for a modular model of cognitive development and functioning that conceives of the various cognitive domains as interacting but independent spheres. In this framework language cannot be accounted for by nonlinguistic cognitive, social, or pragmatically based approaches. Proponents of this view see language as an independent cognitive system based on domain-specific structural principles (Chomsky 1975, 1980; Piatelli-Palmarini 1980, 1987; Fodor 1983).

Even with the advent of new approaches to cognitive development such as information processing (for instance, Caramazza 1986; Kelley 1967; Anderson 1975; Klein 1976), the same types of questions arise: Are there horizontal across-the-board abilities that occur in various modules of the system, or is each module governed by autonomous, unique rules?

This study addresses these basic issues and questions by exploring the linguistic and nonlinguistic cognitive abilities of a mentally retarded young woman named Laura, previously known by the case name "Marta."[1]

Laura's performance profile reflected a dramatic contrast between complex linguistic abilities and markedly depressed nonlinguistic cognitive abilities, with a testable IQ in the low 40s. Her case is a crucial addition to the small but important list of studies that give evidence for the dissociation of language from other cognitive abilities.

Laura's high language–low nonlanguage profile is not one usually associated with the retarded. It has often been observed that as the level of retardation increases, so do the incidence and degree of language handicap (see, for example, Jordan 1967; Wing 1975; Spreen 1965a,b; Blount 1968; Schiefelbusch 1963; Graham and Graham 1971; Karlin and Strazzulla 1952). Quantitative analyses of the speech of mentally retarded children have revealed that such children often exhibit impoverished vocabularies and less complex sentence structure. Relationships between sentence length and mental age (Goda and Griffith 1962; Mecham 1955; Schlanger 1954) and between vocabulary size and mental age have been described (Mein and O'Connor 1960; Wolfensberger, Mein, and O'Connor 1963).[2] (Cromer 1974a reviews the diverse findings of various studies.)

Laura has the converse profile, her linguistic abilities being relatively more intact than her nonlinguistic cognitive capacity. This profile is not often observed. The literature on "savants" documents individuals born with apparently selectively superior abilities in memory, music, calendar calculation, and art (O'Connor and Hermelin 1987, 1989; Viscott 1970; Miller 1987; Hill 1975, 1978; Howe and Smith 1988; Hurst and Mulhall 1988; Selfe 1977; Morishima and Brown 1976), but there have been no recorded cases of savants with isolated linguistic abilities.

Although individuals with *superior* language alongside depressed cognition have not been identified, those with *relatively* intact language have occasionally been found. Evidence for the dissociation of language from other cognitive systems has begun to accumulate in studies of both normal and nonnormal individuals. For example, the presence of linguistic knowledge in advance of cognitive knowledge has been documented by Leonard (1975) and Bloom (1973), who describe children who used semantically empty forms to produce two-word utterances, reflecting incipient syntactic abilities in advance of purported prerequisite semantic or conceptual abilities. Bohme and Levelt (1979) have found that children acquiring German exhibit knowledge of grammatical gender prior to knowledge of conceptual gender. Such data counter the view that language acquisition basically consists of learning how to express linguistically what one already knows nonlinguistically (Schlesinger 1971, 1974; Slobin 1973; Nelson 1974; Bloom 1970; Bowerman 1973a,b; Brown 1973).

A dissociation of language or at least aspects of language from nonlinguistic cognition has also been demonstrated by studies of developmentally impaired individuals such as Turner's syndrome females (Money 1964; Money and Alexander 1966; Garron 1970; Silbert, Wolff, and Lilienthal 1977; Yamada and Curtiss 1981), hydrocephalics (Tew 1979; Schwartz 1974; Swisher and Pinsker 1971), Williams syndrome children (Thal, Bates, and Bellugi 1989), and mentally retarded individuals with unknown etiologies (Curtiss and Yamada 1981; Curtiss 1988). In case studies of a 9-year-old Turners' syndrome girl (Yamada and Curtiss 1981) and of a 6-year-old retarded boy (Curtiss and Yamada 1981; Curtiss 1982) both were found to possess grammatical abilities that outstripped their nonlinguistic abilities. In some of these studies not all aspects of language have been observed to be equally enhanced. For example, in some studies of hydrocephalics and Turner's syndrome females, syntactic ability may be quite developed while semantic ability is reported to be more limited, resulting in "cocktail party speech" (fluent and verbose speech that often conveys little meaning). Retarded and/or autistic children with selectively intact reading skills or "hyperlexia" have also been described (Silberberg and Silberberg 1967, 1968; Eliot and Needleman 1976; Huttenlocher and Huttenlocher 1973; Siegel 1984; Cossu and Marshall 1986; Whitehouse and Harris 1984).

Empirical studies have also disputed claims that social-interactive factors can wholly account for language learning (Snow 1972, 1977; Snow and Ferguson 1977; Dore 1974; Bruner 1974, 1975; Ochs and Schieffelin 1979; Zukow, Reilly, and Greenfield 1979). Blank, Gressner, and Esposito (1978) report on a study in which a child was able to learn the structural aspects of language but failed to use language communicatively. Additional evidence that grammatical knowledge can exceed pragmatic knowledge (or emerge in its absence) comes from certain high-level autistics who exhibit syntactic ability but use language in an inappropriate or limited fashion pragmatically (Ricks and Wing 1976; Tager-Flusberg 1981).

Studies of such selectively impaired individuals add to evidence already provided by research with adults in aphasia and in dementia (Schwartz, Marin, and Saffran 1979; Irigaray 1967; Bayles 1979; Whitaker 1976) that the various components of language are separable from one another and from other aspects of cognition.

1.2 Laura's Case

Laura's case is notable in several respects. First, a wealth of data was collected over a protracted period in a variety of settings to obtain as valid and reliable an estimate of Laura's abilities as possible. Her parents' written documentation of her early development was an invaluable supplement to the professional observations and evaluations made over the years. Second, Laura's cognitive deficits were more pervasive and severe than the deficits of other recently studied subjects. Other subjects have shown a more circumscribed nonlinguistic disability. For example, as I understand it, many Williams syndrome children seem to have a visuospatial deficit rather than an across-the-board, generalized retardation (Bellugi, Sabo, and Vaid 1988). Third, Laura's linguistic ability, particularly her syntactic ability, was more advanced than that of many previously studied subjects (such as those cited in Curtiss and Yamada 1981, and Yamada and Curtiss 1981). Thus, the discrepancy between her linguistic and nonlinguistic capacities were especially marked. Fourth, Laura, nearing the end of adolescence during the study, was no longer undergoing significant developmental changes in either linguistic or nonlinguistic domains. In contrast to certain other young subjects, she seemed to have attained the apex of her development in all areas, making it possible to explore just how far language can progress in the face of significant cognitive limitations.

As the following chapters will show, Laura's case supports a modularity model. Her profile refutes the contention that cognitive, social-interactive, and perceptual factors can account for language acquisition and supports the notion that language is a highly evolved, specialized human ability driven at least in part by a set of principles seen in no other cognitive domain. In addition, this case shows that various aspects of language are separable and differentially related to nonlinguistic abilities.

The value of using single case studies to support or refute a given theory has been well argued by Caramazza (1986). In fact, according to Caramazza, single case studies of the impaired are preferable to group studies in order to make valid inferences about the structure of cognitive systems. In defending the use of single case studies, Caramazza points out that a different theory is not created for each case studied. Rather, various case studies from both normal and nonnormal individuals, taken together (not averaged), provide crucial evidence for or against a given model.

Chapter 2, details Laura's case history and behavioral description. Chapter 3 outlines the methodology used in assessing her abilities. Chapters 4 and 5 detail Laura's language and language use (pragmatics), respectively. Chapter 6 describes Laura's nonlinguistic performance and chapter 7 outlines her performance on neuropsychological and neurolinguistic tests. Chapter 8 discusses the findings and the implications of this profile for views of the relationship between language and cognition.

Chapter 2
Case History and Family Background

When I first met Laura's parents in October 1979, they described Laura, then 16 years old, as an enigma. She had always been developmentally delayed, and despite years of special schooling and tutoring she was generally functioning at a prekindergarten level. She could not read, tell time, give her age, count, or do simple problem-solving. Her language, however, was rather well developed. In fact, she could talk a veritable blue streak, and often did, very loudly and inappropriately. In public it was difficult for the family to be unobtrusive. Laura would speak out loudly, frequently about some seemingly irrelevant point, repeating the same thing over and over, interrupting the flow of conversation among her parents and three normal older sisters.

Many of Laura's problems were evident from an early age, according to her parents, who provided numerous details of their daughter's life. Information regarding Laura's childhood was also obtained from her mother's diary notes, covering Laura's life from age 1½ to nearly 8, and from the extensive medical and educational records that document Laura's early development.

Laura was born on September 12, 1963, following a normal, relatively problem-free pregnancy, the fourth and youngest daughter of a university professor and a teacher.

Her mother recalled that during labor with Laura she herself hyperventilated and "went numb all over" and that at birth the baby was "trembly." However, the attending physician apparently said nothing of any perinatal problems. Laura's mother described her as a limp, floppy, quiet infant, almost "too good."

Both parents noticed developmental delays within the first year (Laura "seemed the same each day") and became concerned when Laura was not yet sitting up at 9 or 10 months. At about 1 year of age Laura was diagnosed by a pediatrician as mentally retarded/developmentally delayed and cerebral palsied with etiology unknown. (The diagnosis of cerebral palsy was later considered erroneous.)

2.1 Developmental Milestones

Laura's developmental milestones were delayed. She sat alone at about 15 months, stood at 20 months, and walked at about 2 years. Toilet training was completed when she was nearly 4 years old. Developmental Quotients of 50 on the Bayley Scales of Infant Development were obtained when Laura was 20, 30, and 41 months old.

2.2 Linguistic Milestones

When Laura was 20 months old, her mother wrote in her diary that Laura understood a few words (*hand, foot, mouth, bath, milk,* and a few others) and that she had used the word *cracker* (/gaka/) for some time but had stopped. She also wrote that Laura "often goes off, seems quite unfocused and unfocusable . . . and it's very hard to chat away to her when she responds so little."

By the time Laura was 2:11, her mother noted that she could say about 15 words, and a developmental specialist's report written when Laura was 3:5 states that, "It would appear that she is very eager to talk. Her parents feel there are 20 words they hear recurrently and that she has used as many as 50 words. Most of the time she uses jargon."

A year later, when Laura was 4:5, her mother wrote, "We're getting more and more whole sentences ("H, get off the stool!").[1] Language development apparently burst forth during the following year.

The same specialist again saw Laura when she was 4½ and reported that she was very mobile and well liked by the teachers. In commenting on her language development, he wrote, "She now talks very much in sentences using plurals and pronouns. She uses few adjectives." He reported that during her visit with him she talked a great deal, naming various items in the room, as well as trying to name a few colors. He judged her to be at the 34-month level in language and social areas.

The inappropriateness of Laura's speech was noted very early on by her mother and later by teachers and specialists. When Laura was about 5:5, her mother wrote the following passage:

> (Laura's) farthest behind area as I see it is social, and a year of some kind of kindergarten might push this along. In that area she might be described as perhaps early three. The other outstanding thing about her in a crowd (other than her plus qualities which I'll go into in a minute) is her inappropriateness of speech. Take her to the shoe store for instance: she'll talk about shoes for

awhile, with much repetition, finding it very hard to wait for the busy salesman. This is appropriate although the loud tones and repetition attract attention. Then when she has the shoes on her feet and her anxiety that she won't get any is relieved and now she has to wait while JB chooses a pair, then begins the perseverations that are *un*related to the occasion. "I eat you," making feint to bite me. . . . "No, you don't," I may reply. "You wouldn't taste good?" she says, and then does the whole thing again. Her other oft repeated conversational filler is pointing to my clothes and saying, "You all flowered [green checked, plaid, or whatever]." This has been for at least a year, many *many* times each day. . . .

2.3   Education

Laura's performance often perplexed educators faced with recommending an appropriate school setting for her.

Between the ages of 2 and 6 Laura attended a school for the cerebral palsied since this was the only one in the area that offered special services to preschoolers. She apparently received speech therapy and occupational therapy while at this school. It was during her stay here, Laura's mother noted, that Laura developed the pattern of "talking quite volubly to no one in particular."

A teacher's report written when Laura was 5½ states that Laura could sight read 15 words and that she knew many letter sounds and all her colors, noting that "the area of number concepts is the most difficult for her . . . her attention span is short—and she will constantly talk of things unrelated to the material at hand." It also states that Laura engaged in "imaginative play usually with hand objects such as cylinders which she used for people while she verbalized aloud." Laura's mother made a similar observation in her diary at this time, noting that Laura could engage in conversation, but generally in her own loud, perseverative fashion.

When she was 6 years old, Laura began attending a full-day child care center that primarily served normal children but accepted a few with special needs. At age 6 she was in class with 4-year-olds and at age 7 with 5-year-olds. When Laura was 6, her mother wrote that she "talks, demanding replies—all the time, often about the same subjects, over and over." An occupational therapist also complained of Laura's "incessant talking, rarely about what we are doing," her tendency to "ramble from subject to subject," and the difficulty in getting her to pay attention to therapy. During this period Laura's

Figure 2.1
Laura at age 6½

mother worked with her on relational concepts such as same/differ-
ent big/little, and one/more-than-one, but had no success. Counting
was consistently difficult for her. In figure 2.1 Laura is shown during
the summer of 1970 at age 6½.

When she was 8, Laura was classified as learning disabled. She
attended a regular K-1 class and received daily individual attention
from a specialist in learning disabilities. In January of that school year
Laura's family moved to France, where Laura attended a day school
for mentally retarded girls. According to her parents, Laura developed a fairly good French vocabulary of at least 100 and possibly up
to 200 words. As indicated in chapter 4, she seems to have retained
at least some of this knowledge.

Following the family's return to the United States when Laura was
9, she was again mainstreamed for a year but then, after further evaluations, was assigned to special schools. At age 11½ she was reclas-
sified as mentally retarded and placed in a class for the trainable
mentally retarded. In an educational system that often correlates linguistic sophistication with intelligence and academic competence,
Laura never seemed to fit neatly into a particular category. When
placed in programs paced to her academic and cognitive abilities, she
was usually linguistically far ahead of the others.

Educational records indicate that Laura's verbal ability was her strong area, whereas her abstract reasoning, her understanding of numbers and numerical operations, and her visuomotor skills were weak. One therapist noted that although Laura's forte was language, her linguistic skill was limited to a very concrete level. She observed that Laura was able to "label and parrot easily" but that when asked to describe pictures, she used only one word or short phrases. When Laura was 8:5, a school psychologist quoted her mother as saying, "Laura has difficulty thinking with her language in the sense that she gives the impression that she knows and thinks more than she really does. This is so because she often repeats what she has heard without understanding the substance of what has been stated." Yet another examiner suggested the possibility that Laura might be an "idiot savant," cautioning against inflated expectations of her potential.

2.4 Standardized Tests

The results of standardized intelligence tests administered to Laura in the past reflect the striking discrepancy that still persists between her verbal and nonverbal abilities (see table 2.1). For example, the spread of at least 20 points between Laura's performance IQ and verbal IQ on the Wechsler tests reveals her relative strength in the verbal area, at least in vocabulary. Moreover, considering that the Wechsler verbal subtests include an arithmetic portion, Laura's verbal and performance levels may be even more disparate than her WISC scores indicate. Subtest scores for the WISC administered in June 1975 at age 11:9 reflect this (see table 2.2).

2.5 Medical Problems

In addition to mental retardation, other medical problems were documented over the years. When Laura was 9 years old, a physician reported the following impressions: hyperkinetic behavior, hypothyroidism, ocular muscle dysfunction with resultant impairment of depth perception and coordination, and precocious puberty (with secondary sexual characteristics appearing at age 8½). He also observed Laura to have a high, arched palate, narrowed maxilla and protuberant upper central incisors, bilateral ankle pronation, and knock-knee deformity. He reported that her attention span was very short and her gross motor coordination poor.

An EEG at age 9 revealed some abnormalities. The report states that the entire EEG was "poorly organized for the age of 9 years with

Table 2.1
Results of standardized tests

Test[1]	Chronological age	Mental age	IQ	Verbal IQ	Performance IQ	Full scale IQ
WPPSI	5:6	—	—	61	44	48
Stanford-Binet	7:5	4:4	55	—	—	—
WISC	9:0	—	—	63	0	45
WISC-R	11:9	—	—	58	0	44
PPVT	12:3	8:11	79	—	—	—
WISC-R	14:9	—	—	52	32	41
PPVT	14:9	6:1	53	—	—	—

1. WPPSI–Wechsler Preschool Scale of Intelligence; WISC–Wechsler Intelligence Scale for Children; WISC-R–Wechsler Intelligence Scale for Children–Revised; PPVT–Peabody Picture Vocabulary Test

Table 2.2
Subtest scores on WISC-R (age 11:9)

VERBAL (IQ = 58)			PERFORMANCE (IQ = 0)		
Subtest	Raw	Scaled	Subtest	Raw	Scaled
Information	8	3	Picture Comprehension	2	1
Similarities	0	1	Picture Arrangement	0	1
Arithmetic	1	1	Block Design	0	1
Vocabulary	24	6	Object Assembly	6	1
Comprehension	10	5	Coding	0	1
	Total:	16		Total:	5

much disorganization in the form of high amplitude, irregular, slow waves, the amplitudes varying up to 150 or 200 microvolts." A tendency toward mild, generalized, paroxysmal activity was also noted. An EEG performed when Laura was 16½ (May 1980) showed spikes in the right temporal region and another performed a month later (June 1980) was also mildly abnormal due to "generalized slowing of the record during the waking stage." However, an EEG done when Laura was 17 (September 1980) and a noncontrast CT scan done when she was 17½ (July 1980) were normal. Subsequent NMR testing was unrevealing.

According to parental and clinical reports Laura began to show some emotional disturbance at the age of 9, and she received psychotherapy for 2 years. The professional who saw her at that time reported that she showed some qualities of a "borderline psychotic," such as dramatic shifts in relatedness and sudden unpredictable and erratic changes of "ego states." However, he stated that he would not call her "blatantly psychotic."

In May 1980, when she was 16½, Laura was hospitalized due to "psychotic behaviors." These behaviors apparently began after she had moved out of her family's home into a residential setting. Her verbal preoccupation with certain themes (death, vomiting), her use of seemingly free associative speech, and a decrease in responsiveness and self-help skills contributed to a diagnosis of schizophrenia. It is important to note that the apparent psychotic behavior was always viewed as secondary to the primary diagnosis of retardation. Over the years Laura was given various medications to treat her behavioral problems and hypothyroidism (for instance, Mellaril, Stellazine, dextroamphetamine tannate (Obotan forte)).

2.6 Environment

Laura lived at home with her family until she was 15 years old. Thus, during her childhood and early adolescence she benefited from an enriched family environment. Laura's parents report that her three normal older sisters played an active, loving role in the raising of their youngest sister, taking her on outings, teaching her, and generally helping to provide her with rich and varied normal life experiences. The family traveled extensively for both business and pleasure, and Laura was always included on such trips.

At age 15 Laura moved to a nearby residential facility at the recommendation of a social worker. She remained in this placement for 1½ years, attending a special school during the day. It was during this time that my study of Laura began. Laura was hospitalized the following year and later was moved to another residential setting. Sometimes she went home on weekends and for vacations, and family members visited her regularly. Until she turned 21 she attended a school for the educationally handicapped during the day.

At this time Laura lives in a residential setting (a group home) but no longer attends school. She and fellow residents participate in special job programs. See figure 2.2 for a photo of Laura as an adult.

2.7 Appearance and Affect

Laura is short (5'1") and sturdily built. During my visits with her she could be unresponsive and lethargic, responding to comments and questions with grunts or monosyllables, or she could be exuberant, almost hyperactive, smiling, clapping her hands, and talking rapidly, almost unintelligibly. Generally she seemed to perk up on outings, whereas in task-oriented settings she was much quieter and more subdued. Even on outings, however, she often seemed relatively oblivious of her surroundings, walking stoop-shouldered, arms crossed, head down. During periods of particular unresponsiveness, her eye contact was poor, and requests to "Look up" or "Look at me" resulted in furtive, rapid, sidelong glances. At other times when she was more alert her gaze was quite steady and sustained. Her moods did not seem to be governed by the presence or absence of medication; she exhibited both behavioral patterns whether she was on or off medication. Often a change in affect occurred within a single session. Laura would be relatively quiet, responding only perfunctorily, when something would trigger a flood of speech. Sometimes it seemed that certain "buzzwords," such as *fat* or *Beatles,* stimulated her logorrhea. At other times the trigger was imperceptible.

Figure 2.2
Laura as an adult

When she was not demonstrating psychotic behaviors, Laura had good self-help skills and with constant prompting could shower and dress herself, comb her hair, brush her teeth, tie her shoes, and so on. However, if left to her own devices, it is doubtful that she would attend to these personal tasks. She could also rollerskate and ride a bicycle. Behavioral observations indicated that she was predominantly right-handed.

Laura was somewhat abnormal in her demonstration of emotion. I sometimes saw her laugh, but rarely in response to a humorous event or comment. Usually she laughed or chuckled when she herself was talking about some past or nonpresent event, showing exaggerated affect and emotion. She sometimes smiled absently but was never able or willing to discuss the reasons for her apparent amusement. When some external event or remark actually gave reason to laugh or smile, Laura often remained serious, apparently unaware of the humor.

When John Lennon was killed, Laura mentioned this fact repeatedly and would say she was sad, but her tone of voice and facial expression did not reflect genuine sadness. In addition, Laura sometimes cried at her residential setting because she said she missed her parents. However, in her interaction with people she often behaved in a detached, unemotional fashion. Sometimes Laura was better at talking about emotions than at actually showing and perhaps feeling them.

Chapter 3
Assessment

Laura's linguistic and nonlinguistic abilities were evaluated through formal testing and informal observation. An extensive number and range of tasks were administered to obtain a comprehensive picture of her mental abilities (see tables 3.1 and 3.2). Testing and observation date from October 1979 when Laura was 16 to July 1982 when she was 18½. There have also been a few subsequent follow-up visits.

As a result, a vast amount of data was collected. Intensive data collection over a protracted period was done to obtain as accurate a picture of Laura's abilities as possible. Many tests that had been given prior to Laura's hospitalization for psychosis were readministered later to ensure a valid assessment of her abilities.

3.1   Test Procedures

Task-oriented sessions generally lasted for approximately 60 minutes, depending on Laura's attention span and cooperation. Except for the month of June 1980 (just after her admission to the hospital), when she was noncommunicative, Laura was generally cooperative. She was usually able to perform at least a few tasks during a given session. Generally when she agreed to attempt a specific task, her performance on that task was fairly consistent from day to day.

Still, Laura was not an easy subject to test. She seemed wary of the task-oriented setting and was often lethargic during testing. She was cooperative to the extent that she pointed to pictures and gave responses, but often her responses were perseverative. Sometimes she seemed to be just going through the motions of responding without really attending to the instructions. In cases where Laura's score on a given test or task varied over several administrations, I assumed the higher score to be a more accurate reflection of her capabilities.

Varying methodologies were used in some cases to further ensure that Laura's linguistic rather than nonlinguistic knowledge was being tapped. At times the methodology for a test had to be modified to

Table 3.1
Language assessment measures
Comprehension Measures
  Curtiss-Yamada Comprehensive Language Evaluation–Receptive (CYCLE-R) (Curtiss and Yamada, forthcoming)
    Phonology, Syntax, Morphology, and Semantics subtests
  Token Test (De Renzi and Vignolo 1962)
  Peabody Picture Vocabulary Test–Revised (Dunn and Dunn 1981)
Production Measures
  Sentence Repetition Battery (Whitaker 1976; Yamada, unpub.)
  Curtiss-Yamada Comprehensive Language Evaluation–Elicitation (CYCLE-E) (Curtiss and Yamada, forthcoming)
  Curtiss-Yamada Comprehensive Language Evaluation–Spontaneous Speech Analysis (CYCLE-S) (Curtiss and Yamada, forthcoming)
  Spontaneous Speech Analysis
  Developmental Sentence Scoring (DSS) (Lee 1974; Lee and Canter 1971; Lee and Koenigsknecht 1974)
Other Evaluation Measures
  Illinois Test of Psycholinguistic Abilities (ITPA) (Kirk, McCarthy, and Kirk 1968)
    Auditory Closure, Auditory Reception, and Auditory Association Grammatic Closure
  Conditional Tasks (Reilly 1982)
  "Easy to see/hard to see" Tasks (Chomsky 1969)

Table 3.2
Nonlanguage assessment measures
Aphasia Test
  Boston Diagnostic Aphasia Examination subtests (Goodglass and Kaplan 1972)
Classification (Inhelder and Piaget 1964; Lovell, Mitchell, and Everett 1962; Curtiss, unpub.)
Class Inclusion (after Inhelder and Piaget 1964; Lovell, Mitchell, and Everett 1962)
Conservation (Fogelman 1970)
  Length (Lovell, Healy, and Rowland 1962)
  Mass (Elkind 1961; Uzgiris 1964)
  Liquid Quantity (Wallach, Wall, and Anderson 1967; Beard 1963)
  Weight (Elkind 1961)
  Number (Wohlwill and Lowe 1962)
Dichotic Listening (Zaidel, no date)
Disembedding
  Preschool Embedded Figures Test (Coates 1972)
  Southern California Figure-Ground Perception Test (Ayres 1972)

Table 3.2
(continued)

Environmental Sounds Recognition Test (Van Lancker, unpub.)

Facial Recognition
  Test of Facial Recognition (Benton et al. 1975)

Familiar Voices Recognition Test (Yamada, unpub.)

Hierarchical Construction–Blocks, Cups, and Sticks (after Greenfield 1978; Greenfield and Schneider 1977; Greenfield, Nelson, and Saltzman 1972)

Logical Sequencing

Gestalt Perception
  Mooney Faces (Mooney 1957)
  Perceptual Integration Test (Elkind, Koegler, and Go 1964)
  Visual Closure (ITPA) (Kirk, McCarthy, and Kirk 1968)

Memory
  Auditory Memory Span Test (Wepman and Morency 1973)
  Auditory Sequential Memory (ITPA) (Kirk, McCarthy, and Kirk 1968)
  Auditory Sequential Memory for Familiar Words (Yamada, unpub.)
  Corsi Blocks (cited in Milner 1971)
  Knox Cubes
  Memory for Auditory Nonverbal Stimuli (MANS) (Curtiss, Kempler, and Yamada, unpub.)
  Memory for Designs (Graham and Kendall, 1960)
  Memory with Verbal Mediation (after Morris 1975)
  Metamemory (Kreutzer, Leonard, and Flavell 1975)
  Visual Sequential Memory (ITPA) (Kirk, McCarthy, and Kirk 1968)

Number Concepts–Counting, Infinity, Magic Show, and Number Recognition (after Gelman and Gallistel 1978; Gelman 1972a,b, 1980)

Representation Abilities
  Drawing (Kellogg 1970; Selfe 1977; Harris 1963; Vereecken 1961)
  Play (Knox 1974; Takata 1974; Florey 1971; Gesell 1940; Gesell and Amatruda 1940)

Rule Abduction
  Muma Assessment Program (Muma and Muma 1979)
  Simple Rule Acquisition (after Furth 1966)

Sensorimotor Abilities–Means-Ends and Object Permanence (Uzgiris and Hunt 1975)

Seriation (after Piaget and Inhelder 1959; Inhelder and Piaget 1964; Lovell, Mitchell, and Everett 1962)

Spatial Abilities
  Copying (Piaget and Inhelder 1967)
  Stereognosis (Laurendeau and Pinard 1970)
  Visual Retention Test (Form C) (Benton 1965)

accommodate Laura's need for constant prompting, or to ensure that her performance wasn't being depressed by nonlinguistic factors. For example, some language assessment tests were administered a second time and Laura was asked to manipulate small figures rather than point to pictures to investigate whether or not picture-pointing was problematic for her.

Still other tests could not be given or completed because of Laura's attentional and cognitive limitations. A tachistoscopic or T-scope test requires the subject to focus on a center point. Since it was felt that Laura could not reliably focus her attention in this way, the T-scope test was not given. The Raven Progressive Matrices (Raven 1951), a nonverbal intelligence test, was attempted, but testing was discontinued since Laura could not understand the task.

A generous dose of verbal praise and prompting was given during each test. In addition, tangible reinforcements were used to keep Laura motivated and attentive. Small food rewards, pictures of the Beatles (her "favorite group"), playing audiotapes of Beatle music, and small token gifts were used to motivate her. Laura also responded to delayed reinforcement, such as the promise of a walk or a soft drink at the session's end. At times Laura showed pleasure and pride that she was doing well. Praise and rewards were given for attention and effort rather than for correct answers.

In addition to conducting working sessions with Laura seated at a table in fairly prototypical task-oriented contexts, I saw her at her parents' home, in her residential settings, in the hospital (where she lived for a year), and at my home. Together we went to coffee shops, restaurants, shopping malls, on walks, and to the zoo. On one occasion Laura spent a night at my home. Thus, I had the opportunity to view her in a wide range of contexts, interacting with loved ones, teachers, fellow students, patients, roommates, strangers, and babies.

Audiotape recordings of each session were made on a Sony TC 142, and transcripts of some of these tapes were used as the data base for the spontaneous language and conversational analyses. My own journal notes provided additional data. An audiotape made by Laura's parents of a family dinner conversation was also transcribed and analyzed.

3.2   Linguistic Assessment

A list of the language measures used is presented in table 3.1.

3.2.1 Comprehension
Laura's language comprehension was tested through administration of the Curtiss-Yamada Comprehensive Language Evaluation–Receptive battery (CYCLE-R) (Curtiss and Yamada, forthcoming), the Token Test (De Renzi and Vignolo 1962), and the Peabody Picture Vocabulary Test)–Revised (PPVT) (Dunn and Dunn 1981). The CYCLE-R covers many structures and features normally acquired between the ages of 2 and 9 (the primary language acquisition years) in the areas of syntax, inflectional and derivational morphology, lexical and relational semantics, and phonology. A description of the receptive battery is presented in appendix A. A brief description of the Token Test is also included in appendix A.

3.2.2 Production
Laura's language production was evaluated by analysis of her performance on imitation tasks as well as by analysis of her elicited and spontaneous speech.

Imitation tasks. Imitation tasks have been given to children (Slobin and Welsh 1973) and to adult aphasics (Whitaker 1976) and have been found to be a useful means of assessing linguistic knowledge. Such tests provide a means of testing the upper limits of an individual's linguistic competence; children have been observed to be unable to imitate utterances beyond their competence (Slobin and Welsh 1973; but compare Bransford and Nitsch 1978). The imitation battery included items described by Whitaker (1976) as well as items I designed myself. Stimuli included sentences and phrases that were either well formed or ill formed syntactically, morphologically, semantically, or phonetically. Laura's task was simply to repeat the utterances.

Elicitation test. The Curtiss-Yamada Comprehensive Language Evaluation–Elicitation battery (the CYCLE-E) was developed to parallel the CYCLE-R. The CYCLE-E includes many syntactic, morphological, semantic, and phonological features covered by the CYCLE-R and certain others as well, such as conditionals and modals. The parallel in the receptive and elicitation batteries makes it possible to assess both comprehension and production of the same features using the same stimuli. See appendix A for a description of the CYCLE-E test format.

Spontaneous speech. Transcriptions of sessions and visits with Laura provided an extensive sample of spontaneous speech. An audiotape made by Laura's parents of a dinnertime conversation was transcribed and added to the spontaneous language data base. The transcriptions were analyzed with attention to the type and range of structures used, productivity, and appropriateness in context.

A quantitative analysis was also performed using the Curtiss-Yamada Comprehensive Language Evaluation–Spontaneous Speech Analysis (CYCLE-S). The CYCLE-S supplemented the qualitative analysis of Laura's speech, offered a means of quantifying the range of structures used, their degree of complexity, and their appropriateness in context.

Laura's speech was also assessed using the Developmental Sentence Scoring technique (DSS) (Lee and Canter 1971; Lee 1974; Lee and Koenigsknecht 1974).

3.2.3   Other Tests

Laura was given particular subtests of the ITPA (see table 3.1) (Kirk, McCarthy, and Kirk 1968), a conditionals test (Reilly 1982), and an "easy to see/hard to see" task (Chomsky 1969).

3.3   Nonlinguistic Assessment

It was important to obtain as clear an idea of Laura's cognitive level as possible, and one means of doing this was to give tests evaluating abilities that have been described in age- or stage-related terms. To assess her level within Piaget's framework, tests associated with the first three stages—the sensorimotor stage, the preoperational stage, and the concrete operational stage—were administered to Laura.

Other abilities that purportedly show developmental progression (such as memory, number concepts, and hierarchical construction) were also tested to determine Laura's performance relative to proposed norms. Many of the nonlinguistic abilities that were examined are hypothesized to be prerequisite to or otherwise linked to language.

In addition, numerous tests were administered to determine whether Laura's pattern of abilities could be accounted for along hemispheric parameters. To this end Laura was given tests tapping abilities that are theorized to be governed by one or the other hemisphere or that are claimed to indicate hemispheric dominance.

Listing the tests given is a complicated matter since there are numerous possible ways of organizing and categorizing them. Some areas have been described in the literature in both Piagetian and non-Piagetian terms (for example, spatial abilities), and some abilities can be cross-categorized. Memory processes, for example, can be examined as developmental phenomena or from a neuropsychological perspective.

The specific nonlinguistic tests administered to Laura are listed in alphabetical order in table 3.2. Many of the tasks are described, also in alphabetical order, in appendix B. They are listed here in the order in which results are discussed in chapters 4 and 6.

3.3.1 Object Permanence and Means-Ends Tests
Object concepts and means-ends behavior were investigated using the Uzgiris-Hunt Ordinal Scales of Psychological Development (Uzgiris and Hunt 1975). (See under "Sensorimotor Tests" in appendix B.)

3.3.2 Conservation Tests
Standard Piagetian conservation tasks for length (Lovell, Healy, and Rowland 1962), mass (Elkind 1961; Uzgiris 1964), liquid quantity (Wallach, Wall, and Anderson 1967; Beard 1963), weight (Elkind 1961), and number (Wohlwill and Lowe 1962) were administered (Fogelman 1970). Sometimes the tasks were modified in minor ways to increase Laura's attention span and motivation; for instance, foodstuffs were used in the number conservation task.

3.3.3 Seriation Test
The seriation task was adapted from Piaget and Inhelder 1959, Inhelder and Piaget 1964, and Lovell, Mitchell, and Everett 1962.

3.3.4 Classification Tests
Laura was given tests for classification and class inclusion developed by Inhelder and Piaget (1964) using a methodology designed by Lovell, Mitchell, and Everett (1962).

3.3.5 Representational Tasks
Play. Play skills were evaluated informally according to measures described by Knox (1974), Takata (1974), Florey (1971), Gesell (1940), and Gesell and Amatruda (1940).
Drawing. Spontaneous drawings were analyzed according to criteria discussed by Kellogg (1970), Harris (1963), Selfe (1977), and Vereecken (1961).

3.3.6 Spatial Abilities Tests
Copying. Laura was presented with a series of 21 geometric designs (Piaget and Inhelder 1967) to copy. The designs tap knowledge of topographical and Euclidean spatial concepts. There are norms from below 2 years of age. In addition, Form C (a copying version) of the Visual Retention Test (Benton 1965) was administered.
Stereognosis. Laura was given the Stereognosis test (Laurendeau and Pinard 1970), which tests knowledge of spatial concepts and re-

lationships in a tactile-visual modality. There are norms for children between 3 and 12 years of age.

3.3.7   Number Concepts Tests
Laura was given the "Magic Show," a means of assessing number concepts in preschool children, developed by Gelman (1972a,b, 1980); a counting task (Gelman and Gallistel 1978); an infinity task modeled after tasks described by Gelman (1980); and a number recognition task.

3.3.8   Logical Sequencing Task
Laura was asked to sequentially organize a scrambled set of two to six pictures to create a story. She was encouraged to verbalize the story created by the picture sequences.

3.3.9   Classification/Categorization Test
Laura was given a test (Curtiss, unpub.) to further assess her ability to make conceptual distinctions that are also marked linguistically (for example, gender).

3.3.10   Rule Abduction Tests
To assess Laura's ability to abduce a rule or rules from limited available data, she was given a Rule/Nonrule Governed Learning test (Muma and Muma 1979) and a Simple Rule Acquisition test (inspired by Furth 1966).

3.3.11   Hierarchical Construction Tasks
Block models and stick models of increasing hierarchical complexity were presented to Laura, who was asked to build identical structures (Greenfield and Schneider 1977; Greenfield 1978). She was also asked to nest a set of seriated cups of various colors (Greenfield, Nelson, and Saltzman 1972).

3.3.12   Aphasia Test
Laura was given subtests of the Boston Diagnostic Aphasia Examination (Goodglass and Kaplan 1972) for auditory comprehension, naming, repetition, automatic speech, and music. Because she could not read or write, subtests requiring these skills were not given (although the word recognition test was attempted to explore whether she might recognize any words).

3.3.13   Memory Tests
To evaluate auditory short-term memory, Laura was given the Auditory Memory Span Test (Wepman and Morency 1973), the Auditory Sequential Memory test from the ITPA (Kirk, McCarthy, and Kirk 1968), and the Memory for Auditory Nonverbal Stimuli test (MANS) (Curtiss, Kempler, and Yamada, unpublished). In addition, to increase Laura's motivation and attention, a nonstandardized word span test was given, consisting of words particularly salient to her (such as *Beatles, fat, cake*).

To assess visual short-term memory, Laura was given the Knox Cubes test, the Corsi Blocks test (described in Milner 1971), the Visual Sequential Memory test from the ITPA (Kirk, McCarthy, and Kirk 1968), and the Memory for Designs test (Graham and Kendall 1960). As mentioned under 3.3.6, she was also given the copying version of the Visual Retention Test (Benton 1965).

Metamemory abilities were assessed by asking Laura questions modeled after Kreutzer, Leonard, and Flavell's interview study (1975), for example, "Would it be easier to remember five things or one thing?"

A verbal mediation test that I designed (after Morris 1975) was given to see whether Laura could use verbal mediation (specifically rhyming) to facilitate recall.

3.3.14   Dichotic Listening Test
Laura was given a dichotic listening task designed by Eran Zaidel of UCLA.

3.3.15   Gestalt Perception Tests
Laura's gestalt perception abilities were examined through administering the Mooney Faces test (Mooney 1957), the Perceptual Integration Test (Elkind 1978; Elkind, Koegler, and Go 1964), and the Visual Closure test of the ITPA (Kirk, McCarthy, and Kirk 1968).

3.3.16   Disembedding Tests
To assess disembedding, also known as figure-ground perception or field independence, Laura was given the Southern California Figure-Ground Perception Test (Ayres 1972) and the Preschool Embedded Figures Tests (Coates 1972).

3.3.17   Facial Recognition Test
Laura was given the Test of Facial Recognition (Benton et al. 1975).

3.3.18   Environmental Sounds Recognition Test
Laura was given an experimental version of the Environmental Sounds Recognition Test (Van Lancker, unpub.).

3.3.19   Familiar Voices Recognition Test
Laura was given an ad hoc familiar voices recognition test that I designed, using voices of Laura's family and friends.

Chapter 4
Language

Various key questions come to mind in considering Laura's linguistic ability. What was the status of her linguistic knowledge? How complex or complete was her grammar? How did her abilities in the various aspects of language compare with each other? In addition, how did her comprehension compare with her production?

4.1 Syntax

4.1.1 Production
Laura revealed an extensive knowledge of English syntax in her language production. Her linguistic sophistication is especially evident in her use of syntactically and morphologically rich structures that are relatively late acquisitions in normal development. For example, Laura used both full and agentless passives.[1]

(1) Ooh, there's a car gettin' ticketed, Dad. That('s) last year at [name of school] when I first went there three tickets were gave out by a (police) last year.

(2) [Talking about her hair]
I got it cut already by a maid.

(3) [Talking about barracudas]
I was never swallowed by one.

The full passive has been reported to be a relatively uncommon, late-appearing structure (Baldie 1976; Horgan 1978; Crystal, Fletcher, and Garman 1976). This form is infrequent not only in child language but also in adult language and in adult language directed at children (Givón 1979, Horgan 1978; Harwood 1959; Brown 1973). Horgan (1978) states that even the 11- and 13-year-old children in her study did not produce the full range of passives. For example, their nonreversible passives (passives in which the action is unidirectional) did not include agentive passives even though agentive nonreversible passives are used by adults. Laura spontaneously produced both reversible and nonreversible agentive passives.

Additional evidence of the complexity of Laura's speech is her use of a wide range of complex sentence structures, that is, structures involving the recursive operations of coordination and subordination. Although the earliest forms of complex sentences begin emerging at age 2 (Limber 1973; Bowerman 1979), some structures are still infrequent at age 5.

In coordination several constituent sentences are linked by a coordinating conjunction. Laura frequently used coordination in her speech.

(4) We're really excited about school starting, *and* I love it myself.

(5) . . . and I enjoyed cooking *but* it's not simple, I know.

In subordination an embedded structure can function to modify a constituent of the sentence such as a noun phrase, verb phrase, or adjective. Let us first examine Laura's ability to modify noun phrase constituents with embedded structures—in other words, her ability to use relative clauses. Though relative clause-like forms begin appearing fairly early (around age 3), it has been noted that the earliest forms do not include *wh*-relative pronouns, subject relatives, or any relative clause attached to the subject NP (Limber 1973). Laura was able to use *wh*-relative pronouns, true object relatives, subject relatives, and double function relatives (double function relatives being constructions like (9) where coreferential NPs serve different, "nonparallel" functions in the main and embedded clauses). In particular, subject and double function relatives are late acquisitions.

(6) She, does paintings, this really good friend of the kids who I went to school with last year, and really loved.

(7) . . . a really nice guy who I went to and I really loved him after a while.

(8) The cook who does it, um sometimes give us these good enchiladas an' oh, they're so good!

(9) I'm very good friends of a girl that cuts (. . .)'s hair, that I'm working with.

(10) He was saying that I lost my battery powered watch that I loved; I just loved that watch.

(11) That's the number that I'm stayin' at.

The multiple embeddings in many of Laura's sentences further attest to her sophisticated syntactic level.

Laura was also able to modify and elaborate the verb phrase through use of subordinating conjunctions of time, causality, and so on. Bowerman (1979) notes that studies have shown children as old as 6 or 7 have difficulty interpreting sentences with subordinating conjunctions like *before, after, when, until, if, because,* and so on. Cromer (1968) reports that *before* and *after* are uncommon even in the speech of 5-year-olds.

(12) I'm waiting *until* my hair grows out.

(13) He's my third principal I've had *since* I've been here.

(14) It makes me feel sad *because* they had to leave.

(15) They just went to a bar *after* the movie was over.

Another form of embedding is complementation, where the embedded structure functions as a major constituent of the sentence. Laura generally used object complementation in her spontaneous speech, as in (10). No examples of subject complementation were observed.

Laura also used infinitival complements ((16) and (17)) and "headless relatives" ((18) and (19)), forms that often come in toward the end of the third year (Limber 1973).

(16) Want me to help you?

(17) It was hard for me to do, but I did it.

(18) That's where my sister JB lives!!

(19) I know what Monday is.

She also used complements containing participal forms, which have been reported to appear later than infinitival complements (Limber 1973).

(20) I love eating meals.

(21) Did you hear about me not going to this school up in Altadena?

(22) I don't like him puttin' paper towels in my mouth.

Additional evidence of Laura's syntactic maturity may be found in her frequent use of temporal adverbials.

(23) During class, I told everybody.

(24) After a while, I gotten tired of it.

(25) And they said, "Well, we want her coming home once a month."

(26) I'm going home for a little while.

(27) I saw her an hour ago.

(28) I got discharged a month ago, Sunday.

Another example of Laura's ability to modify and elaborate upon simple sentence structure is her use of modifiers or adjectives. She was noted to use up to four modifiers.

(29) Very scary news.

(30) a little round thing from the union

(31) a good friend's second friend

Laura's capacity to use elliptical utterances reflects her sophistication in another area of the grammar. Grammatical ellipsis involves the deletion or omission of sentence constituents that are redundant within the linguistic and/or extralinguistic context. Ellipsis, it is claimed, provides cohesion in the flow of natural discourse. In addition to knowing how to produce more complete utterances, the language user somehow knows that shorter, more fragmented utterances are sometimes permissible and preferable. According to Bloom and Lahey (1978), ellipsis does not appear until after the child has begun to use three-constituent utterances. Laura revealed an understanding of the rules governing ellipsis both in spontaneous conversation (as in (32)–(34)) and in her responses on the CYCLE-E (as in (35)).

(32) E: Who has shorter hair?
     L: I do.

(33) L: Look, what is that? [Showing her own protruding stomach]
     E: [Teasing] That's a baby.
     L: No, it isn't.

(34) Yeah, my dad was all upset and so was I.

(35) E: This clown doesn't have a flower, but this clown ——.
     L: Does.

Laura's responses on sentence imitation tasks reflected her ability to distinguish between syntactic well-formedness and ill-formedness.

(36) J: An apple was eaten by Jeni.
L: An apple was eaten by Jeni.

(37) J: Laura was eaten by an apple.
L: Laura was eating an apple.

(38) J: The horse ran gate through the
L: The horse ran through the horse

(39) J: Cake some here is still
L: [Softly] Cake some . . .

(40) J: I bacon eggs toast for breakfast.
L: It is toast for breakfast.
J: I bacon eggs toast for breakfast.
L: I have toast for breakfast.

(41) J: The apple was eaten by the
L: [No response]

Laura was able to repeat well-formed sentences, as in (36). In contrast, when presented with syntactically or semantically ill formed sentences, she usually either made a change toward a more grammatical string or refused to respond altogether. Such structures seemed strange to her, as reflected by the fact that her responses were often delayed, hesitant, and mumbled under her breath.

Yet more evidence of Laura's sophisticated productive abilities in syntax and morphology comes from her score of 16.7 on the Developmental Sentence Scoring test, which places her above the 90th percentile of the 6:11 age level, the ceiling of the test (Lee 1974).

4.1.2 Comprehension
To determine whether or not someone truly understands the semantic relationships embodied by a particular syntactic structure, it is useful to administer formal receptive tests that isolate the structure from contextual cues. However, although formal tests are often an efficient means of probing linguistic competence, the test-taking situation sometimes conflicts with the very young child's or retarded individual's mode of interacting. The receptive language tests in the CYCLE battery were designed with the cognitive, attentional, and motivational limitations of the cognitively immature or deficient individual

in mind (Curtiss and Yamada, forthcoming). Tests are brief, arrays are simple, pictures are interesting yet clear, and generally only pointing responses are required. In the standardization done thus far, children aged 2 and even younger were found to attend to and succeed on selected tests. Thus, Laura should have had no trouble on the tests with regard to nonlinguistic task demands.

Laura's overall performance on the CYCLE battery of syntax subtests was quite poor. Results of formal testing are given in table 4.1. She showed mastery level performance on only 2 of the 15 subtests for which there are norms, Double Embedding I and Simple Modification. She performed at or below the 2-year-old level on 10 of the 15 subtests.

She did the same or worse on the object manipulation versions of the various tests (Active Voice Word Order, Passive Voice Word Order, *Wh* Questioning of Subject and of Object, and relativization tests). However, her responses on these tests did offer some insight into her performance. In response to a test question, Laura often did not manipulate all of the objects mentioned in the test sentence; she might, for instance, manipulate only one out of two. Her responses thus indicated that she was responding to only part of the test sentence.

It is difficult to conclusively attribute these responses to failure to understand the linguistic structures tested, to processing (for instance, memory) limitations, or to motivational or attentional deficits. Possibly all factors played a role.[2]

In spontaneous speech Laura produced a wide range of structures, many of which she failed to respond to correctly on the comprehension tests. For example, although she did poorly on comprehension tests dealing with word order distinctions, in her own speech she consistently used word order to mark grammatical relationships.

Taken together, Laura's performance on the comprehension tests and her spontaneous linguistic performance give a picture of her linguistic knowledge. In some cases Laura showed the ability to understand and use a structure appropriately and meaningfully in context but did poorly on the formal receptive test. In spontaneous conversation it is probable that nonlinguistic and extralinguistic contextual cues sometimes aided Laura, veiling her lack of understanding of certain constructions. In certain cases, however, such as with passives, she seemed to understand the structure even though her test performance failed to reflect this (see (36), (37), (105)). In cases where Laura did poorly on a given test and was also observed to use the structure in question inappropriately in her expressive language, it is likely that she in fact did not have linguistic mastery over that particular form.

Table 4.1
Comprehension test results: Syntax

Test	Percent correct[1]	Age level[2]	Normal age of mastery[3]
Active Voice Word Order[4]	63	3	4
Be Passive Voice Word Order–Agentive	0	2	5
Be Passive Voice Word Order–Nonagentive	40	<2	4
Clefting	0	<2	>8
Complex Modification	60	2	4
Complex Negation	40	2	4
Double Embedding I[5]	**80**	**4**	**4**
Double Embedding II	20	3	7
Get Passive–Nonagentive	40	<2	4
Object Relatives	40	2	8
Object Relatives (with Objects)	20	no norms	no norms
Simple Modification	**100**	**4**	**2–3**
Subject Relatives	60	2	4
Subject Relatives Ending in N–V	20	4–5	8
Wh Object Relative Pronouns	40	no norms	no norms
Wh Questioning of Object	20	<2	5
Wh Questioning of Subject	60	2	4
Wh Subject Relative Pronouns	80	no norms	no norms

1. Laura was given a score for percent correct on each test given. Based on normative data, each score was then translated into an age equivalent score. On the most recent version of the test battery most subtests tap each target structure or feature 5 times. A score of 4 or 5 correct (80%–100%) is considered evidence of "mastery."
2. Laura was assigned age level scores for specific subtests on the basis of normative data. For example, if Laura attained 40% correct on a given test, the age at which the majority of children received 40% correct was considered her age level equivalence.
3. The "age of mastery" for a given structure is the age at which 80% or more of the normative population attained scores of 80% or better.
4. Some of the subtests Laura was given had more than five items at the time of administration (most CYCLE subtests have since been revised to contain five items each). Thus, her percentage scores on some CYCLE subtests do not reflect uniform 20% increments in performance. In these cases the criterion of 80% or better performance is still used as an indicator of mastery.
5. Laura could earn an age level equivalence above the age level of mastery on a given test if, for example, she had a 100% score, 80% of 7-year-olds performed at the 80% level, and only 80% of the 8-year-olds, the oldest normals tested thus far, averaged 100%. In this case, although the age of mastery is 7, Laura would earn an age level equivalence of 8.

To obtain another measure of the sophistication of Laura's grammar, she was tested for comprehension of structures that are reported to emerge only after age 5: *John is eager to see* versus *John is easy to see* (Chomsky 1969). Though both structures have similar surface forms, their underlying structures differ. To understand this structure, the child must become aware that in the second sentence *John* is the object rather than the subject of the main clause.

Chomsky and others have found that it is only after age 5 that children come to understand referential relations in complement clauses lacking overt subjects. In *Julie is easy to see* the subject of *easy to see* is unspecified. The sentence can be roughly paraphrased as "Julie is easy for anyone to see." Young children typically assume that in this sentence *Julie* is the subject of *see* and that it is Julie who is doing the seeing. Thus, when shown a blindfolded or "sleeping" doll and asked whether it is easy to see or hard to see, the young child will typically say, "Hard to see," even though the doll is in plain sight. Other studies have replicated Chomsky's finding that children initially interpret *Julie* as the logical subject of the infinitive in *Julie is easy to see* (Cambon and Sinclair 1974; Cromer 1970, 1972, 1974c; Kessel 1970).

When shown the blindfolded doll and asked whether it was easy or hard to see, Laura answered, "Hard to see," thereby giving the answer typical of very young children. When asked to "Make her easy to see," Laura not only took off the doll's blindfold but also held the doll very close to her own eyes. In this case her answer was ambiguous, since she treated the doll as both the subject and the object of *easy to see*. However, when she was asked, "Why was the doll hard to see before?" she said, "Because she had bad eyesight." This is reminiscent of the egocentric responses of 5-year-olds reported in later studies of comprehension of these structures (cited by Karmiloff-Smith (1979)). Apparently children of this age interpret *easy to see* as "easy for me to see," whereas children of about 8 understand that *easy to see* means "easy for anyone to see."

Since researchers have found that the blindfold, because of its salience, may steer the child toward the incorrect response, the task was repeated using the same doll without the blindfold. In the modified task the doll was placed lying down on the table in front of Laura, so that its eyes were closed. The same test questions were asked. Laura again stated that the doll was "hard to see," and when asked to make it "easy to see," Laura stood the doll up so that its eyes opened. She again cited "bad eyesight" as the reason why the doll was originally "hard to see." When asked "What did you do to make her easier to see?" she cryptically responded, "Good eyesight."

Again, judging from her action of standing the doll up so that it could see better, she apparently considered the doll to be the logical subject of the infinitive, a response typical of younger subjects.

Thus, Laura did not show particular sophistication in this area. As far as I know, she did not produce *easy/eager* constructions in her spontaneous speech.

The Token Test (De Renzi and Vignolo 1962) is considered to be a highly sensitive measure of auditory language comprehension and has been used with aphasic adults and language-disordered children (as discussed in Whitaker and Selnes 1978). This test assesses the ability to understand sentences of varying syntactic complexity without the benefit of nonlinguistic contextual cues (see appendix A for task description). Norms are available from several abnormal populations (see, for instance, Zaidel 1977; Swisher and Sarno 1969; Tallal 1975) as well as from normal adults and children from age 3 to grade 6 (DiSimoni 1978).

Laura did poorly on this test, scoring 17 out of 39. The mean score for children from 3:0 to 3:6, was 19.55. De Renzi and Faglioni (1978) have used a similar version of the Token Test to define four levels of impairment in aphasics. Laura falls within the severely impaired category, reflecting the low level of comprehension that she demonstrated on this test. She was able to do all the items in sections A and B but began missing items in section C. When asked to "Show me a large green square," for example, she pointed to the large green circle. Given that Laura showed knowledge of squares, circles, and color and size words on the shorter, simpler items in sections A and B, it appears that it was the longer and more complex instructions that posed difficulties for her. Lesser (1976) has claimed that reduced auditory memory is a performance limitation characteristic in aphasics. As will be shown in chapter 6, auditory memory was also a problem for Laura, an interesting finding given that she was able to produce such lengthy utterances.

4.2 Morphology

4.2.1 Production

Laura produced many morphologically complex forms and showed knowledge of many grammatical distinctions signaled morphologically and lexically. Her performance on the CYCLE-E indicates that her grammar included rules for marking singular/plural agreement on the auxiliary.

(42) E: And here these sheep . . .

     L: are jumping.

(43) E: Now you tell me about the girl . . .

     L: She is jumping.

On the sentence repetition task her spontaneous inclusion of the omitted auxiliary also reflects this knowledge.

(44) E: He thinking about you.

     L: He's thinking about you.

In the same task she also spontaneously corrected errors in subject-verb agreement marking on the main verb.

(45) E: He wear his shirt.

     L: He wears his shirt.

Examples from Laura's spontaneous speech further reflect her ability to mark agreement on verbs.

(46) The girl arrives . . .

(47) Santa comes in the roof.

(48) They know us . . .

(49) They take trash up.

In addition, she correctly used singular and plural noun forms on the CYCLE-E (as in (50)–(52)) and in her spontaneous speech (as in (53)).

(50) E: Here are two . . .

     L: tubs.

(51) E: But here is just one . . .

     L: cup.

(52) E: Here are two . . .

     L: watches.

(53) They got this really nice gold thing, these things.

Another appropriately used morpheme in Laura's speech was possessive-*s*.

(54) That's my father's last name . . .

(55) head leader's friend

Laura also demonstrated knowledge of the auxiliary system. She used the tense/aspect markers *will*, *-ing* and *-ed* both on the CYCLE-E (as in (56)–(57)) and in spontaneous speech (as in (58)–(60)).

(56) E: Now you tell me about the cat.

   L: He is sleep*ing*.

(57) E: But here the girl already . . .

   L: Walk*ed* away.

(58) [We hear people speaking a foreign language (not Spanish) nearby]

   They're speak*ing* Spanish, can you hear it?

(59) [L has gone upstairs to show to her dad a prize we've given her and has just returned]

   I show*ed* my dad.

(60) [J and L are getting already to go to the zoo. J, still in night-clothes, says she has to get dressed]

   L: [Amused] You can't go like that. They*'ll* kick you out.

Laura also used some complex auxiliary forms.

(61) *I've been* there three years since *I've been* a student.

(62) I *should've* brought it back.

(63) Maybe I *could* play with friends.

(64) . . . and I didn't know how much money (. . .) the bank *would* let me take out of my account.

Laura had sorted out the irregular present and past forms of *be* and *have*, correctly marking the verbs for person and tense.

(65) I was 16 last year, now I'm 19 this year.

(66) I'm really glad they're back here now.

(67) I think that night we were going disco or something . . .

(68) My dad was all upset.

(69) Just the second friend I've ever had.

(70) It has like three rooms.

(71) Be better if I had a little respect.

(72) She had the ruined watch.

Laura asked few questions, but when she did, she appropriately inverted the order of the subject and auxiliary (or copula), assigning tense marking correctly.

(73) *Did you* know my dad's in the hospital?

(74) *Are we* going on an outing today?

(75) *Are you* sick?

(76) *Is it* her day off?

(77) What *should I* do this afternoon?

(78) What's *the apple juice* for?

(79) What *are you* doing Thanksgiving?

4.2.2 Comprehension

Laura failed to achieve a level of mastery on many CYCLE-R tests for morphological forms that she used in her own speech. Of the 11 morphological forms examined through formal testing, Laura attained mastery level on only two, Comparative *-er* and Tense/Aspect Marker *-ing* (see table 4.2).

One intriguing finding is that Laura performed better on the test for lexically marked verb phrase pluralization (singular/plural is marked on the auxiliary) than on the test for inflectionally marked pluralization (singular/plural is marked on the main verb). Whereas she scored 80% for singular agreement on the auxiliary singular test, she scored only 20% for singular agreement on the verb singular test.

Laura's poor performance on comprehension tests of various morphological forms seems to indicate that her knowledge of such forms was limited. It is intriguing that she spontaneously used some of the same forms. As mentioned earlier, various aphasic syndromes are marked by a patient's capacity to produce grammatically correct structures despite poor comprehension (Whitaker 1976). However, although Laura's comprehension can be said to be reduced, it was certainly not absent, as an examination of her semantics attests.

4.3 Semantics

To determine to what extent Laura's production could be said to exceed her comprehension, it was crucial to examine her understanding

Table 4.2
Comprehension test results: Morphology

Test	Percent correct[1]	Age level	Normal age of mastery
Comparatives	100	4	4
Noun Pluralization			
Singular	33	2	4
Plural	75	2	4
Possessive-*s*	50	4	7
Superlatives	0	2	4
Tense/Aspect			
-ing	80	5	5
-ed	40	<2	6
Verbal Singular/Plural (marked on auxiliary)			
Singular (*is*)	80	5	5
Plural (*are*)	40	2	>8
Verbal Singular/Plural (marked on main verb)			
Singular (*-s*)	20	<2	5
Plural	40	2	>8

1. Refer to notes for table 4.1

of the meaning of the various linguistic structures and features she used. As will be evident in the examples to follow, it was definitely not the case that Laura lacked all comprehension of linguistic input and of the words and structures she used. Such a profile would be no more theoretically interesting than the linguistic skills of a mynah bird or parrot. Through the study of transcortical aphasics, it has been shown that ties between linguistic output and cognitive functioning can be severed in the mature individual. The present case offers the more rare opportunity to look at the relationship between linguistic and cognitive functioning in development. As will become evident, Laura seemed to grasp the meaning of many words she used, though she apparently understood others only partially and still others minimally, if at all.

The word *semantics* has been used in different ways in the language acquisition literature. *Semantic knowledge* refers to cognitive knowledge that is expressed in linguistic terms (Bloom 1973; Schlesinger 1974; Bowerman 1974; Dore 1975). Some researchers define the term very broadly, seeming to equate semantic knowledge with conceptual knowledge. They describe children at the prelinguistic or the one-word stage as expressing "semantic intentions" or "semantic functions," where nonlinguistic behaviors (such as eye gaze, reaching, or pointing) and context can combine with single words or with one another to form "semantic relationships" (Ingram 1971; Antinucci and Parisi 1973; Greenfield and Smith 1976).

Others hesitate to assign a relational semantic structure to a word on the basis of its occurrence in a nonlinguistic context (Bloom 1973; Schlesinger 1974; Dore 1975). In this view, ability to sort pictures on the basis of certain perceptual or conceptual features (for instance, length versus flatness) would not in and of itself be considered a semantic ability. However, demonstrated knowledge that one particular noun classifier should be used with words for long things and another should be used with words for flat things would be considered to reflect a semantic distinction. As Bowerman (1976, 110) aptly puts it, "Cognitive discriminations are not automatically also semantic ones. They assume significance only when they become linked to one or another aspect of language." This more restricted use of the term *semantics* is adopted for the purposes of this study.

4.3.1 Production

Laura's spontaneous utterances reflected that she had correctly sorted out the meanings of many forms and could use them appropriately.

In English the concepts of gender, animacy, person, and number are marked on pronouns. In using pronouns correctly, one must be able to mark these nonlinguistic concepts in a linguistic way. Laura was able to do this. She used various subject pronouns appropriately, marking the pronouns for gender, number, and person.

(80) [Referring to her mother putting up Christmas stockings]
She would like nail it.

(81) [Describing a picture of a man lifting a baby]
He's lifting up somebody.

(82) [Re her sister and herself]
Well, we walked on the beach a bit.

(83) J: Oh gosh, you are so lucky.
L: That's what they said.
J: Who said that?
L: M'folks did.

Similarly, Laura seemed to have sorted out the meanings of various object pronouns.

(84) [Sneezes and needs a Kleenex]
Would somebody get me a Kleenex?

(85) [Re a woman speech therapist]
I saw her an hour ago.

(86) [Re a phone call to her dad]
I asked him about Thanksgiving.

(87) [L has just mentioned that she has gone to a doctor's appointment. J mistakenly assumes that the physician is male]
J: Did they, he look at your eyes?
L: No.
J: Your mouth?
L: [Pause] It was a her.

(88) [Re looking for a new car with her parents]
And when we went looking around and his Victor guy found us, this blue car.

In spontaneous conversation Laura also frequently used inanimate *it* appropriately.

(89) [Re a picture of an apple with a bite out of it]
It got bitten halfway.

(90) S: Is there something special about wearing blue today?
L: You just wear it anytime.

(91) [Re a camera]
The flash on it didn't work.

(92) J: The *Muppet Show*'s good.
L: Yes, my granddad used to watch it.

Laura's responses to semantically anomalous utterances on the sentence repetition task reveal that she was aware of the feature of animacy.

(93) J: The book is very happy.
L: The book is very happy. *People* are kind of happy.

J: Can a book be happy?

L: A person can.

(94) J: The pencil can't see very well.

L: The pencil can't see very [laughs] *eyes* could see.

One could argue that Laura's reaction to the anomalies in such sentences reflects her awareness of the range of probable events in her everyday experiences rather than her knowledge of abstract semantic features (such as ±animate, ±human) per se. Of course, it is probable that most language users are not consciously aware of such abstract features as they speak.

Only occasional errors in pronominal selection were noted.

(95) The air, she rise . . .

One might argue that Laura was using the feminine pronoun here for metaphorical effect. It is difficult to judge this since Laura uttered this sentence during one of her long stretches of speech that was not entirely appropriate in context.

Correct use of pronouns reflects syntactic as well as semantic knowledge. Not only did Laura use the appropriate forms to mark various semantic features, she seemed to be able to use pronouns appropriately according to their syntactic role in the sentence (such as subject or object).

Laura generally used possessive adjectives correctly as well.

(96) That's where my sister lives.

(97) [Re her male principal]

Alls you have to do is go into his office.

(98) [J is asking L to talk about a previous occasion, when L visited J's home]

J: And then what did you do? Do you remember?

L: Went to your house.

Other concepts Laura was able to mark in her speech were negation (as in (99)–(100)) and temporal notions of past and future (as in (101)–(103)).

(99) I don't have a roomer. My roommate left. Alexandra left.

(100) [Re Halloween]

I didn't dress up as anything. I just went to school as my regular self.

(101) [Re having eaten all her lunch]

I'm finished. I'm done.

(102) [S and J are trying to get L to draw her family]

S: I wanna see the rest to your family [that is, wants L to draw them].

L: [Apparently thinks S means "in person"]

Oh, they're gonna be home.

(103) [J and L are getting ready to go to the zoo. J says she has to get dressed]

L: [Amused] You can't go like that. They'll kick you out.

4.3.2 Semantic Relationships

Laura's semantic knowledge extended beyond knowing the meaning of particular lexical and inflectional morphological markers. For example, Laura was able to use passive structures appropriately (see (1)–(3)), and her performance on sentence repetition items indicates that she also understood the semantic relationships implied by the passive structure (see (104) and (105)).

She seemed aware that such notions as agents, object, and patient do not have invariant syntactic roles (in other words, that subjects are not always agents and in fact may sometimes be objects or patients) and that active and passive structures signal different relationships between NPs and verb.

(104) J: Can an apple be eaten by a stove?

L: No, apples are eaten by people!

(105) J: Laura was eaten by an apple.

L: Laura was eating an apple.

4.3.3 Lexical Semantics

Laura's facility with language was also reflected by her knowledge of vocabulary items that one would not expect of someone with an IQ in the low 40s.

(106) J: Bachelors are married.

L: No, they live alone.

(107) J: What does it mean to be a genius?

L: Smart.

(108) J: What does it mean to be retarded?

L: Not smart.

Generally retardation has been associated with a poor or impoverished vocabulary (Mein and O'Connor 1960; Wolfensberger, Mein, and O'Connor 1963).

In spontaneous interaction Laura used words that reflect a relatively specialized (even sophisticated) vocabulary. One day Laura said, "A belly dancer, it means, 'Far Eastern dance.'" Laura's interest in words is particularly evident during a family dinner conversation taped prior to the beginning of this study. In the interchange (see appendix C, dialogue 3) Laura asks for synonyms for using a "low voice." Upon seeing a picture of a bear, Laura didn't simply say, "Bear"; she was able to give two more specialized terms, "Polar bear" and "Kodak" (presumably for Kodiak) (see (109)). Similarly, when shown a bus she didn't simply say, "Bus"; instead, she answered, "Touring bus" (see (110)). When asked to name as many fruits as she could, she was able to name only a few (with much prompting), but one was "pomegranate" (see (111))! She was also able to give a number of synonymous phrases for the notion "go to sleep."

(109) [Shown a picture of a bear]

Polar bear, like in the word, "Kodak." [Kodiak?]

(110) [Shown a picture of a bus]

Touring bus.

(111) [J has asked L to name as many fruits as she can]

Pears . . . apples . . . pomegranates.

(112) [S and J are trying to elicit the phrase "go to sleep"]

S: Go to . . .

L: [Gestures sleeping, flat palms together, head resting on back of one palm]

S and J: [Ask for "words"]

L: Zonk out.

Sack out.

In the above examples Laura exhibited at least some understanding of some of the words. However, a significant feature of her speech was her propensity to use forms whose meaning she did not seem to grasp fully.

(113) [L rote counts to eleven (with help) and lauds herself]
Hey, Laura! You're really smart. You've really worked on that address.

(114) "Jack," that's my father's last name, "Jack."

(115) J: Tell me a joke, Laura.
L: Go jump in a lake.

Laura's limited understanding of the notion of "joke" is further illustrated by her own telling of a joke. The following "joke" is similar to that of a preschooler.

(116) An' he told such a taco joke! An' he tol' me this, OK. It's about this taco, an' the taco eats the meat, and the [laughs as she talks] ta' (unintelligible) over (unintelligible) told a joke.

Particularly interesting was Laura's propensity to use temporal and numerical terms in her spontaneous speech. It was evident that although she had learned the subcategorization rules governing the insertion of the "right kinds" of elements into the "right kinds of places" in the sentence, she often didn't know the full meanings of the terms she used and the phrases she constructed.

The mismatch between Laura's linguistic and conceptual knowledge is well illustrated by her use of numbers.

(117) J: How many nights did you stay there? [At a hotel with her family]
L: Oh, about 4 out of 1.

(118) I was 16 last year and now I'm 19 this year. [L had just turned 16 when she made this comment]

(119) It's ten of nine. [Actually it was four after ten]

Although she was able to use as many as four adjectives in a given noun phrase, she perseveratively used the same numerical terms to modify, particularly the cardinal terms *two* and *three* and the ordinal terms *second* and *third*.

(120) It takes me two hours to get to [name of residential home] where I live.

(121) These two dogs kept going after me.

(122) It has like three rooms.

(123) Well, I think my mother's gotten three notes . . .

(124) I did my third year at [name of school].

(125) . . . 'cause this is like, my third home.

(126) I said I got two friends in there.

(127) . . . I think I brought my camera wi' me that week. That was an old one. That was like my third, the one a friend gave me was my third one. . .

In some cases the numerical references are clearly nonfactual. For example, the statement "It has like three rooms" referred to Laura's parents' home, a large two-story house with many more than three rooms. In many cases Laura seemed to have simply plugged a numerical reference into an appropriate sentence slot without regard to meaning.

Similarly, it sometimes appears that Laura knew where temporal adverbials belong in a sentence but did not really understand their specific meanings.

(128) It's a week from Saturday and JB, A, an' my mom 'n dad— I think I brought my camera with me that week.

In (128) Laura used a future adverbial in a sentence where she was clearly talking of a past event.

During acquisition, normal children also mismatch temporal adverbials with verbs when they become aware of adverbials but do not yet have a command of their meanings, as in "I had a bath tomorrow" and "We will do it yesterday" (Ames 1946). I have noted specific examples of this in the speech of my own children.

[Aaron (age 2:3) wants to get out of the shopping cart]
I wanna get out this Tuesday!

[We're in the car and Jason (age 3:4) is impatient to go home. It's Saturday evening]
Jason: Mom, I wanna go home on Thursday.
J: When do you wanna go home?
Jason: Tomorrow.
J: Do you wanna stay here all night?
Jason: No, I wanna go home Thursday.
J: So you wanna stay here for five days?
Jason: [Emphatically] Now. I wanna go home now.

Additional evidence that Laura used adverbials she did not fully understand came from her use of nonfactual statements (as in (129)) and idiosyncratic temporal forms (as in (130)–(132)).

(129) I got discharged [from the hospital] a month ago Saturday. [At this time she had been discharged for many months]

(130) One's got married, a week. [A week ago?]

(131) She just died, she died a month. [A month ago?]

(132) Oh, frack, we finally got that new Mexican 'cause 'is flights came in Wednesday month.

Laura did not always use temporal adverbials erroneously. Note (118), for example, in which she used past tense *was* with *last year* and present tense *am* with *this year*. She also correctly used the terms *tomorrow*, *yesterday*, and *now*. One might of course question whether she really knew the meaning of, say, *last year* and *this year*, since often statements she made containing these terms, though syntactically correct, were factually wrong ("I was 16 last year and now I'm 19 this year," a statement made when she had just turned 16).

Another indication that Laura used phrases she did not fully understand came from her performance on a sentence repetition task. Whereas Laura was reluctant to repeat syntactically anomalous "sentences," she often had no problem repeating semantically anomalous sentences where the temporal adverbial and the verb tense did not match. She readily repeated the following sentences, for example.

(133) A week from Thursday I saw you.

I will see you a month ago.

Last week I will see you.

4.3.4   Comprehension

In conversation Laura sometimes responded appropriately to the situation. A discussion Laura and I had following her overnight visit at my home was particularly revealing because I had a clear idea of what had actually happened and thus whether her answers were correct. Sometimes her responses reflected semantic and conceptual awareness.

(134) [We're discussing L's overnight visit at my home]

J: We came and we picked you up right, Friday afternoon. And then what did we do? Do you remember?

L: Went to your house.

(135) [At the zoo]

J: What do you want to go see?

L: Crocodiles.

However, often the responses were not factual. In the above case Laura said she wanted to see the crocodile, but when we went to see it, she didn't want to look at it (actually, it was an alligator). Later, when we talked about what we had done at the zoo, we had the following exchange:

(136) J: Well, did you tell them [people at her residential setting] what we did?

L: Went to the zoo.

J: That's right. Did you tell them what we saw?

L: A crocodile.

J: A c . . . you didn't wanna see the crocodile. There was an alligator there, but remember, you didn't wanna see it? Remember?

(137) [Talking about L's overnight visit]

J: Before we went to my house, on Friday, where did we go? You remember, we were in the car and we drove someplace.

L: The zoo.

Laura's answer in (137) was incorrect. We went to the zoo on Saturday after she had slept over. Only after additional questioning and prompting did she answer correctly.

(138) [Still talking about L's overnight visit]

J: Do you remember what we bought [at the grocery store]?

L: Apples.

J: That's right, we bought some apples, what else did we buy? Remember? We bought some other stuff. At the store, what was it? What were the things that we bought? It's now three days since we did that, so you should be able to remember. [L did not respond to any of the above questions] Laura, what else did we buy at the grocery store?

L: Apples.

J: Apples, and what else?

L: Chicken. [A correct response]

The distinction between Laura's semantic and conceptual knowledge is revealed in many examples. Often Laura used words and phrases that fell within the correct semantic category or domain (a location, a date, a number, and so on). However, to make correct comments and responses, conceptual knowledge is also required. In many cases Laura gave the appropriate type of response to a question, but her response was factually incorrect. This was particularly evident in comments and responses involving time and number concepts. Referring to her sister A, for example, Laura once remarked, "She's the oldest." A in fact is the third of the four sisters in Laura's family.

(139) [J has just given L two pennies]

J: How many pennies do you have now?

L: Five.

(140) J: Is your dad married?

L: Yes.

J: To whom?

L: [Mother's name] Two years ago.

J: When?

L: Two years ago.

(141) J: What is your phone number?

L: 794-4488. [Not her real number, or even close]

(142) J: So, September 2nd, and how old were you on your last birthday?

L: I think I was 19 when I changed dates. [L was 16 when she said this]

(143) S: What year is this?

L: It's 1976 because Nixon threw up. [It was actually 1980]

(144) S: What month is this?

L: This is 1977. [It was actually 1980]

Laura's responses sometimes also reflected limitations in her general knowledge.

(145) J: What country do you live in?

L: [Name of town in which L's parents reside]

(146) J: Who's the president of the United States?

L: President Lordy. [A neologism?]

There was a wide scatter in Laura's performance on formal comprehension tests in semantics. Aspects of her performance were reminiscent of normal albeit delayed developmental patterns. For example, she did better on object pronouns that are acquired earlier than on ones that are acquired later. Other features of her performance were unusual or "deviant" rather than simply delayed. For example, although she did well on *in front of, in back of, next to*, and *under*, she did poorly on *in* and *on*, which are acquired earlier in the normal child.

Laura did poorly on many tests for which the age of mastery is as low as 2 years of age, but she did well on a few tests for which the age of mastery is 7 or 8 (for instance, *who* versus *what; for/with*). See table 4.3 for a summary of her performance.

Laura also did poorly on the Peabody Picture Vocabulary Test (PPVT), attaining a mental age of only 3:11. Whereas vocabulary was one of her greatest strengths when she was a young child, her failure to adequately increase her vocabulary as she grew older may account for her decreasing level of performance in this area. Her low score on this test is also interesting in view of her use of specialized words in spontaneous speech.

Table 4.3
Comprehension test results: Semantics

Test	Percent correct[1]	Age level	Normal age of mastery
Before and *after*	could not do		5
Case-Marking Prepositions			
for/with	100	8	7
to/from	80	5	3
of/by	20	4	6–7
Disjunction (*or*)	could not do		4
It vs. Other 3rd Person Pronouns (−animate)	0	2	6
It vs. Other 3rd Person Pronouns (+animate)	40	4.5	6
Lexicon: Description II	40	2	2–3
Lexicon: Description III	80	2	2–3

Table 4.3
(continued)

Test	Percent correct[1]	Age level	Normal age of mastery
Locative Prepositions			
in front of/in back of	80	5	6
next to/under	80	5–6	6
in/on	22	2	2
Object Pronouns			
me/you	80	4	2–3
him	33	2	2
her	67	2	2
us	0	2	7–8
it	0	2	6
them	0	2	5–6
Possessive Adjectives			
her	100	7	3–4
his	100	6	3–4
my	100	8	4
your	100	8	4
our	0	2	6
their	0	2	5
Quantifiers			
one	40	2	4
many	20	2	5
none	40	2.5	4
every	100	4	2
some	20	3	5
all	80	2	2
a	20	no norms	
a few	20	no norms	
lots of	80	no norms	
Simple Negation	100	3–4	2
Subject Pronouns			
(*he, she, they*)	60	5	6
Tense/Aspect			
finish	40	2	2
gonna	0	2	7
will	20	2	7
Who vs. *What*	80	7.5	8

1. Refer to notes for table 4.1

4.4 Conditional Tasks

Conditionals were interesting to explore since their understanding and use seems to require the integration of syntactic, morphological, and semantic knowledge. Given that Laura's syntactic and morphological abilities seem to outstrip her semantic and conceptual abilities, I wondered to what extent this would be reflected in her understanding and use of conditionals.

Although the first conditional or conditional-like structures begin emerging as early as 2½ years of age, children often do not master the complexities of this structure until they are 8 or older (Reilly 1982). Reilly found that the emergence and development of conditionals involves a complex interaction between conceptual and linguistic abilities that is revealed in the child's linguistic behavior during the years from 2 to 8.

Although 2½-year-old children have not yet mastered the complex morphological features associated with conditional structures in English, they are already capable of conveying notions associated with the conditional, such as antecedence and consequence. As they grow older, they elaborate and refine both their conceptual and their linguistic knowledge to understand and produce a variety of conditional constructions. Reilly notes that the relationship is a complex one; at times conceptual development is ahead of linguistic development and vice versa.

Though she did not show comprehension of counterfactual questions (see (147)–(148)), Laura's responses to hypothetical and generic questions were generally appropriate.

(147) J: What if this lion had been a pig?

L: Eat like a pig.

(148) J: What if this lion's face had been a monster face?

L: A bear is scary.

Perhaps the distinguishing feature for Laura was that the ability to mentally project a situation that is not logically possible was conceptually more difficult than thinking about a situation that is logically possible.

With regard to hypothetical conditionals, Laura's type of response was characteristic of children age 5 and older in Reilly's study.

(149) J: What if you ran across the street without looking?

L: You would get hit by a car.

(150) J: What if you get a bad cut?

     L: If I had a cut I would find a Band-Aid.

Younger children generally responded with present antecedent and future consequent clauses, for instance, "If I *have* a bad cut I *will* get a Band-Aid." Only the older children seemed able to deal with the notion of possibility as opposed to simple predictability and to mark it morphologically.

In Reilly's study an additional interactive task was designed to further explore the subject's understanding of conditional structures. On this "Lion's Face" task the evaluator and subject take turns constructing a lion's face (with construction paper pieces) and saying, "If you put the X on, I'll give you a jelly bean" (X = nose, eyes, and so on). Laura did poorly on this task. She could not produce antecedent and consequent clause structures and instead gave simple imperative commands, "Put the mouth on." Even then, her comments were simply repetitions of part of the experimenter's utterance from the previous turn ("If you put the mouth on, I'll give you . . .").

In contrast to this low level performance, Reilly found that one 2½-year-old in her study could produce the full target form:

[Kate (2:10)] If you put on a eye, I'll give you a jelly bean.

On imitation tasks Laura generally repeated back only the final clause of the stimulus sentence, a response not commonly noted in normal children (Reilly 1982).

(151) J: If the sun comes out, the snow will melt.

     L: The snow will melt.

(152) J: If I were a raccoon, I would live in a tree.

     L: I would live in a tree.

On the rare occasions when I could get her to repeat the antecedent clause, she generally omitted the word *if*, even after several attempts to get her to repeat it.

(153) J: If I were fat,

     L: If I were fat, pregnant.

     [J does many repetitions; L only repeats, "I were fat . . ."]

     J: I'd be on a diet.

     L: I'd be on a diet.

(154) J: If I had been fishing,

     L: I had been fishing,

J: I would have caught the biggest fish.

L: I woulda caught the biggest fish.

When the sentence was broken into two parts, she had no trouble repeating the phrases, including past perfect and pluperfect forms. Her limited auditory memory span may be relevant here. Perhaps she simply could not keep the lengthy stimulus sentences in mind.

Of interest with regard to Laura's understanding of such structures is her response in (153), where she spontaneously said, "If I were fat, pregnant." Given that she meant, "If I were fat, I'd be pregnant," it is evident that she had not yet completely mastered the semantics of such structures (and possibly the conceptual relationship between fatness and pregnancy!).

There are few conditional or conditional-like structures in Laura's spontaneous speech samples and those that do appear do not clearly indicate that she knew the meaning of such structures, although examples (149) and (150) indicate that she did have some understanding.

(155) If her Timex breaks, that's it.

(156) The place where I get my hair cut!, pays an hour if it's a woman, I think, if it's a man it pays, he pays, five hours, I think, of work, he pays . . .

4.5   CYCLE–Spontaneous Speech Analysis

The CYCLE–Spontaneous Speech Analysis (CYCLE-S) offered a means of measuring Laura's linguistic knowledge quantitatively. The CYCLE-S morphosyntactic analysis indicated that Laura's abilities in this area were superior to her semantic and pragmatic knowledge. Laura used a wide range of structures and features: of 62 possible grammatical categories included for analysis on the CYCLE-S, Laura used 56, or 90%. Her error rate for these categories was 2.7%. This is better than the 51 categories (82% of the total) used by two normal children, Colleen (7½) and Michael (8½), whose language was analyzed for comparison. Of 24 syntactic operations analyzed (negative marker placement, equi-NP deletion, subordinating conjunctions, and so on), Laura made only 2 errors, compared with Colleen's 10 and Michael's 1.

Laura used 22 of the 24 semantic categories included on the CYCLE-S. Her error rate was somewhat higher in the semantic area than in the syntactic area. Two samples of approximately 50 utterances analyzed yielded slightly different error rates: 6% and 9%. In contrast, normal children studied thus far made virtually no semantic errors.

4.6   Productivity

In considering the significance of Laura's unusual language abilities, we must ask whether her language is truly productive. Are her complex utterances merely rote memorizations or formulaic, stereotypic strings? Certain factors show this not to be the case.

Errors are one strong indication that Laura's utterances were novel forms. Many errors Laura made were similar to those observed in normal children.

(157) Now this is my (in) fact third home I've ever have lived in.

(158) There were a Timexes.

(159) Three tickets were gave out by a police last year.

(160) [Re her watch]
       It was gaven a month by this friend.

(161) I don't know how I catched it.

(162) The parents of her are from Peru.

(163) These are two classes I've tooken.

(164) [Item on CYCLE-E]
       J: But here the candles have . . .
       L: been litten.

Also common were errors that are not characteristic of normal language learners. For example, sometimes Laura omitted major sentence constituents in her utterances.

(165) It makes me feel sad because they had to leave, 'n [stops abruptly]

(166) She was so mad at.

(167) I think (picked up) the VW that, day.

(168) J: Who lost 50 pounds?
       L: I did at the wedding, I didn't eat my appetite (. . .) my appetite was like (at the) time.

Other utterances were simply uninterpretable.

(169) And what hot air is rosen it, the air, she rise; and air, air if you're really are (innocent) air, in fact the air is behind us . . .

(170) She was thinking that it's no regular school, it's just plain old no buses . . .

The unusual form and/or content of a number of Laura's utterances make it highly unlikely that she heard others use the same structure.

(171) It's somebody (with) brown hair, somebody (that) has his bangs trimmed in Iceland.

(172) Oh, frack, we finally got that new Mexican 'cause 'is flights came in Wednesday month. They didn't get a erkier [ɚkiɚ], erka [ɚkə], erkee [ɚki], that new guy . . .

(173) I ate slow 'n went to the beach.

(174) You see, so that's where they been, the mother's accent spits right out the mouth.

(175) Well, we were talking a walk, my mom, and there was this giant, like, my mother threw a stick.

Laura's ability to create novel, function-changing forms (for instance, through nominalization) also reflects the productive nature of her grammar.

(176) F: What about the problem of you and cussing, Laura?
      L: Well, big upsetness!

(177) We went car-looking.

(178) A new recoveress came to [name of city college].

(179) I don't have a roomer, my roommate left.

(180) An' the lady, the Bullocker, very young that cuts hair. [Bullocks is a chain of department stores in California]

Of particular interest is the fact that Laura was sometimes linguistically perseverative. Some often repeated phrases were "I was so surprised," "I'll never forget (remember) that," "Look at my fat," and "Who killed John Lennon?" Such utterances were not echolalic per se, since many were repetitions of her own rather than someone else's utterances. Many of the formulaic expressions Laura used were permeable rather than "frozen"; elements within the phrases were analyzable and subject to change.

Laura's frequent use of stereotyped words and phrases made it appear that she simply plugged certain items into structure, "mad libs" fashion. (In the game of "mad libs," players are asked to volunteer words of varying categories (noun, verb, adjective, and so on). These words are then plugged into blanks in a story. The results are usually hilariously nonsensical.)

One day Laura told us that the principal of her school had died while eating lunch on the lawn at school. That same month her father reported that Laura had told him Susie and Jeni had died while driving to San Diego. We were struck by the structural similarities of these two stories:

Principal//died//while eating lunch//on lawn at school

S & J//died//while driving//to San Diego

A study of Laura's transcripts revealed that Laura often used particular phrases. The examples in each following group are taken from various transcripts; they were not consecutive utterances.

(181) I heard the principal came back.

I heard United broke down.

I heard my psychologist is back.

I heard it's very sad news about . . .

I've heard it's very scary news about . . .

(182) It was really surprising.

I was really surprised.

A week ago I was so surprised.

(183) Mrs. Smith, my principal died.

Well, my grandmother died, in Minshin. [Michigan]

. . . Lady Aplarent just died a month.

. . . I've had [name of school] principal 'n she died.

. . . 'n this teacher died, in school.

(184) What's that guy's name?

The mother of um, what's that girl's name?

Really get the thing, the, what do you call it?

I think it was in, what was that town . . .

Laura's most complex, voluminous output was produced during lengthy stretches of speech that could aptly be termed "spiels." These spiels contained many examples of complex structures that seem quite normal out of context. However, in context many of the utterances are uninterpretable. Although individual sentences might be well formed, connections between utterances are often unclear. The spiels contain many stereotyped or perseverative chunks and phrases, unclear anaphoric references, frequent topic switches, neologisms, and imprecise articulations. There are many false starts and hesitations, and the speech is punctuated by unintelligible items. Many words and phrases within these spiels were therefore difficult or impossible to transcribe.

There were times when Laura seemed a little more intelligible and comprehensible, but she was much less talkative at those times and her speech did not exhibit the rushed, headlong quality that it did during the spiels.

Below are several examples of spiels. (Additional examples of Laura's speech are included in appendix C.)

(185) It was kind of stupid for dad, an' my mom got um three notes, one was a pants store, (of) this really good friend, an' it was kind of hard. An' the police pulled my mother out of (there) an' told the truth. I said, "I got two friends in there!" The police pulled my mother (and so I said) he would never remember them as long as we live! An' that was it! My mother was so mad!

(186) It's like a flight I came from. Out of our time, which was like, what time it was [question intonation] when we were arriving. It was one-thirty. An' I set it back from the very wrong time. (They got messed around with a [píla˞]), on that, too much (or) messed with it. Kinda went, it's not electric, it used ta do, "buh" that (sun), he got me, when I was visiting somebody . . . an' she just died, very sudden(ly) (. . .) an' she gave me this really nice, it was gold . . .

Much of this is reminiscent of the speech of a Wernicke's aphasic. Compare the above passages with the ones reported by Gardner (1976):

Gardner: What brings you to the hospital?

Wernicke's aphasic: Boy, I'm sweating, I'm awful nervous, you know, once in a while I get caught up, I can't mention the tarripoi, a month ago, quite a little, I've done a lot well, I impose a lot, while, on the other hand, you know what I mean, I have to run around, look it over, trebbin and all that sort of stuff.

Gardner: Thank you, Mr. Gorgan. I want to ask you a few—

Wernicke's aphasic: Oh sure, go ahead, any old think you want. If I could I would. Oh, I'm taking the word the wrong way to say, all of the barbers here whenever they stop it's going around and around, if you know what I mean, that is tying and tying for repucer, repuceration, well, we were trying the best that we could while another time it was with the beds over here the same thing . . .

Between these two interchanges, Gardner writes, he "attempted several times to break in, but was unable to do so against this relentlessly steady and rapid outflow." This spiel-like quality is similar to Laura's speech.

Perhaps the use of stereotyped phrases and formulae enabled Laura to speak with a superficial fluency, given that the range of ideas and topics she could or would discuss was limited. It has been argued that normal speakers incorporate routines and automatic phrases in their conversational speech (Pawley and Syder 1980; Kempler 1977; Van Lancker 1975) and what such routinization enables us to speak fluently and rapidly without having to constantly construct our utterances "from scratch." We have a sizeable repertoire of prescribed phrases that we can retrieve during speech to reduce the energy and effort required for formulating sentences. Laura, too, had a repertoire of speech formulae that she called upon, but her set seemed more limited than that of a normal speaker. In addition, she paid little attention to meaning and appropriateness in her use of these formulae.

Of course, the claim that normal individuals use stereotyped forms in discourse does not preclude the need to account for the ability to use language productively and creatively, but merely gives some insight into the processes involved in fluent speech. Similarly, Laura's use of stereotyped forms does not diminish the productive nature of her linguistic ability.

4.7 Phonology

Laura's phonological knowledge was not extensively examined in this study, but a few observations were made.

4.7.1 Production

Laura showed a sensitivity to the sounds of language and on a number of occasions mentioned that someone had an accent or was speaking another language.

(187) My principal's from Germany. That's why he has an accent.

(188) [L overhears people speaking a foreign language]
       They're speaking Spanish, can you hear it?

On occasion she attempted to show off her foreign language skills.

(189) J: Laura, can you count for us? One . . .
       L: Un, deux, trois, cinco, six, (. . .) I could understand but no Spanish. (. . .) Spanish, I have French.
       J: Can you count in English for us?
       L: One, two, three, four, . . .
       J: Can you count any more after that?
       L: Undo, quato, cinco, ses.

Note the mixing of French and Spanish and the quasi Spanish words.

As mentioned in chapter 2, Laura's family spent a year in France when Laura was 8 years old. At that time she apparently picked up some French words and learned some French phonology. Laura's mother made a list (in the diary) of Laura's French words which indicates that Laura did not actually acquire knowledge of French syntax, but instead learned only words and phrases. Vestiges of this knowledge still remained at the time of this study.

(190) S: How do you say your name in French?
       L: [lóʁa] boy that name, which I've tooken, um in France, which is called, "madame," [mədǽəm] an' "woman" in France is "muhdum" [mədʌ́m]. Like the accents . . .
       S: What are men called?
       L: They're called "monsieur" [məsijɚ], "monsieur" [məsijɚ].
       S: Very good!
       L: Very good French I've every spoken, lived in there. I should know some.
       S: Well you used to know a lot of words.
       L: We used to, I used to. Yeah, so Rheims [ʁɛ̃s] is kinda nice, France . . .

She was able to pronounce *Rheims* fairly accurately. In addition to being aware of French phonology, Laura was aware of differing stress patterns of the words (as in *monsieur*).

In English Laura's production of isolated words was fairly normal although in connected speech she tended to mumble and slur words and her intonation and pause patterns were bizarre at times.

4.7.2 Comprehension

Laura performed at a 5-year-old level on the Curtiss-Yamada Comprehensive Language Evaluation–Phoneme Discrimination Measures (CYCLE-P). Of the 156 illustrated minimal pairs presented to her, Laura correctly distinguished 143 pairs (91.7%) and made 13 errors. Her errors may reflect her lack of knowledge of some of the vocabulary items on the test (for example, *muscle* versus *muzzle*). Normal children given the CYCLE-P made fewer than 10 errors at age 6 and fewer than 5 errors at age 8.

4.7.3 Auditory Closure (ITPA)

On the Auditory Closure test the examiner reads a word with syllables or sounds omitted and the subject must guess the word on the basis of this incomplete input. Some examples are *airpla/, tele/one, re/ ig//ator*. This test taps part-whole perception through use of verbal elements. That is, upon being presented with a part, the subject must project the whole on the basis of this partial information. This ability seems linked to phonological knowledge in that in order to project a whole word from a part, the individual must have an underlying representation of the word and an awareness of the possible elements that can fit into particular "slots" within the word.

Laura's raw score on this test was 18, giving her an age score of 6:1, the highest age-level score she attained on the ITPA subtests she was given. This score contrasts with her preschool level performance on the nonlinguistic part-whole perception tests. Thus, Laura's part-whole perception for linguistic input seemed better than her perception of nonlinguistic input.

4.8 Summary

An examination of Laura's language reveals its rich and complex character, particularly in the areas of syntax and morphology. Expressively she was capable of producing forms and structures characteristic of a child at least 5 years of age or older. Some indicators of the sophisticated level of her grammar are her use of passivization and various complex structures including complementation and subordination. In spite of their complex structural qualities, however, Laura's utterances were sometimes semantically anomalous.

Many of Laura's semantic difficulties reflected problems in lexical semantics. Recall, for example, her erroneous use of the term *address*.

(191) [L rote counts to eleven (with help) and lauds herself]

Hey, Laura! You're really smart. You've really worked on that address!

In most cases Laura's semantic errors seemed to reflect her conceptual deficiencies. Her conceptual difficulties with number and time (see chapter 6) made it hard for her to associate the appropriate linguistic terms with the appropriate concepts.

It is notable that Laura's conceptual limitations did not preclude her learning at least some of the structural properties of the linguistic terms. She was able to figure out where to use certain linguistic forms within a sentence despite her cognitive limitations. Thus, syntactic knowledge appears to be more independent of conceptual knowledge than semantic knowledge.

Of course, *semantic level* and *cognitive level* are not synonymous. There was also a gap between Laura's semantic and conceptual knowledge systems. Significantly, Laura's productions reflected her special talent for sorting out lexical items semantically and for using them in appropriate locations, as illustrated by her use of semantically and syntactically well formed utterances that were factually incorrect. Thus, when asked who the president was, Laura could name *a* president, or when asked when an event happened, she could name *a* point in time. That is, Laura's responses often fell within the correct semantic category or domain, indicating that she was aware of some of the semantic features associated with the question or answer. However, because of her conceptual limitations she often could not provide responses that were factually correct.

Thus, although her semantic knowledge may not have been as enhanced as her syntactic and morphological knowledge, her ability to pick up specialized vocabulary items was likely also a reflection of her particular talent for acquiring linguistic knowledge.

Laura's language was definitely productive, as shown by her ability to create novel utterances and by her production errors, which often looked very much like those made by normal children in the course of language acquisition. Other errors were quite unusual.

Laura's feel for phonology was yet another indication of her facility with language. Her performances on the CYCLE-P and on the Auditory Closure test of the ITPA were relatively better than her performances on many of the other tests.

Thus, as her performance in various linguistic areas indicates, Laura displayed a special talent for acquiring language.

Chapter 5
Pragmatics

Pragmatics has been described as the study of the rules governing the use of language in context (Bates 1976; Rees 1978). In the 1970s, just around the time focus was shifting from syntactically to semantically based studies in language acquisition, there was also an increased emphasis on the study of the social-interactive or pragmatic factors governing and influencing language. The shift away from a theory appealing to abstract linguistic categories reflected the increasing sentiment that to fully understand language, communicative functions and the context in which language occurs must be considered (Halliday 1975; Campbell and Wales 1970). The significance of pragmatics is also highlighted by claims that pragmatic factors affect and shape language change (Givón 1979). Givón and others (see Slobin 1977) have pointed out that processes observed phylogenetically also operate ontogenetically. For example, child speech, like unplanned discourse, is marked less by complex embedded structures and more by coordination and repetition.

The dependency between grammatical structure and social-interactive variables has been described in various ways (Shatz 1982). One view claims that language structure is laid down on a pragmatic base, so that the child's task in language acquisition is to map form onto previously established communicative functions (Bruner 1975; Garnica 1978; Macnamara 1972, 1977; Zukow, Reilly, and Greenfield 1979). Another view claims that the structure of conversation facilitates language acquisition. In this view, sequences of dialogue provide a framework for the learning of various structural operations. In the process of being exposed to the question-answer cycles, reformulations, expansions, and so on, that occur during discourse, children purportedly learn the various substitutions, deletions, and transformations that operate on structures (Snow 1972, 1977; Keenan and Schieffelin 1976; Newport 1977).

Many pragmatically based arguments address only certain aspects of language, especially the earlier acquired forms. However, in the early 1980s efforts were made to account for formal categories in adult grammar within a functional framework (see, for instance, Bates and MacWhinney 1982). Although some have characterized functionalism as being antithetical to innatist views, others point out that the functionalist camp contains both nativists and empiricists. Bates and MacWhinney (1982, 177) for example, state that "it is also possible to view the functionalist approach as a particular type of genetic determinism, albeit via an indirect causal route."

Hopper and Thompson (1980) and Givón (1979) have discussed the notion that certain syntactic structures and the rules governing them—for instance, main and subordinate clauses, passives, and topicalized and elliptical structures—are functionally motivated and can only be accounted for by reference to function. Another communicative function said to motivate the form of complex structures is the need to distinguish between old and new information (as in topicalized sentences) and between foregrounded and backgrounded information (Hopper 1979).

Stylistic variation, pronoun use, and deixis (of person, place, and time) are also putatively motivated by communicative or functional considerations. For example, knowledge of when to use *you* or *me*, *here* or *there*, *recently* or *soon* is claimed to be governed by pragmatic context; the perspective of the speaker and the listener govern and influence the linguistic form.

Laura demonstrated an awareness of many discourse conventions and features such as turn taking, responses to questions and comments, elaboration of a topic, and requests for information. At times Laura could participate in a relatively normal interchange (see appendix C). However, she often failed to make use of the necessary discourse conventions. Conversing with Laura was frequently an odd, unpredictable experience. Sometimes she remained silent except for monosyllabic grunts in response to questions and comments, and then suddenly started off on one of her spiels, either in response to someone else's comments or triggered by some unseen, internal stimulus.

On these occasions she failed to follow conversational rules such as those defined by Grice (1975). Grice posits a *conversational principle*, namely, "Make your conversational contribution such as is required at the stage at which it occurs, by the accepted purpose or direction of the talk exchange in which you are engaged." He also proposes four subrules or maxims of this principle:

Quantity: Be as informative as is required, but not too much so.

Quality: (1) Do not say what you believe to be false. (2) Do not say that for which you lack adequate evidence.

Relevance: Be relevant.

Manner: Be perspicuous. (1) Avoid obscurity and ambiguity. (2) Be brief and orderly.

Laura violated all four subrules. The quantity of her speech was not well controlled; the truth value of her utterances was often questionable; and much of her speech was irrelevant and obscure.

To some extent Laura was able to use pronouns anaphorically.

(1) [Re a recent doctor's appointment L has just mentioned]

J: Did they, he look at your eyes?

L: It was a *her*.

(2) Her parents are all Armenian, *they* don't speak English.

(3) There's the principal's office and there's the clock that *he* uses.

(4) Well, I've gotten a different teacher and I loved *her*.

(5) My hair was, 'bout, well, last time I had *it*, cut, *it* was here [pointing to her neck].

However, in many instances her reference was unclear.

(6) J: You seem a little sad today, Laura.

L: It's a little sad *they* have left. An' I told the head leader *they're* not sure if (they're) gonna set it for, for eight, eighth, our time which will be as, [abrupt pause] our time an', the girl arrives where it's one, which is in school right now.

In addition, Laura's interchanges were often inappropriate and unrelated to the topic at hand.

(7) J: You have, you have a savings account?

L: Yessss!

J: How do you earn your money?

L: Well, we were taking a walk, my mom, and there was this giant, like, my mother threw a stick.

J: Wait, Laura, is that, are you telling me how you earned your money?

> L: No, we were taking the money to, my trip. To, uh, Eureka, or something, to fly or something.

Sometimes there was a logical connection between Laura's response and the preceding remarks. Unfortunately, Laura did not always clearly establish the connection for the listener. For example, on several occasions when we were discussing new cars Laura began talking about going to the dump.

(8) J: How are your mom and dad?

    L: They're just fine.

    J: Really?

    L: They got a new car!

    J: What kind?

    L: Blue.

    J: How nice! Is it a big one?

    L: Yeah, it's a station wagon.

    J: A station wagon?

    L: Yeah. [Shivers with excitement and claps]

    J: Wow, then they can take you places in it!

    L: To the dump, maybe.

    J: Where?

    L: To the dump.

    J: [Mystified] To a dump?

    L: Yeah, you can dump trash.

    J: Why would you wanna go to a dump?

    L: We have.

Laura's parents later explained that new cars and dumps were in fact related. When they had their old van, the family occasionally drove to the local dump to dispose of things like old appliances. These trips were apparently a great adventure for Laura. Now that the old van was gone and the family had purchased a new car, Laura was probably worried that such trips would no longer be possible. Our discussion of the new car had consequently prompted her remarks about the dump. However, Laura failed to communicate pertinent information that would make the connection between the two topics apparent to the listener.

It was difficult to follow Laura during many conversations.

(9) [J is explaining to L the plan for the day's session. L just begins talking]

L: I might get my bangs (. . .) trimmed, 'cause this friend, of my mom's is away, my mom's haircutting, go to the airport, 'n my haircutting came in! An' so we haven't made one yet. Just to get [gesturing cutting at the back of the head] back (. . .) here, 'n one [k]! y, know, [k] (. . .) really get the, thing, the what do you call it.

S: The hair, the scissors?

J: The scissors?

L: I was goin' there, cross the street where I live it's right across from, (. . .) this is

S: From your new, from where you live now?

L: Yeah, an' it's really nice, me 'n this friend went there, an' I went there an' I'm [sort of sings] gra-du-ating from, it! I'm (. . .) [Slaps self]

S: You're now what?

J: What are you?

L: (I think it's, they) go up to fifty an hour, a dollar an hour an' um,

S: Hm. A new class you mean, or a new place?

L: It's no, the place where I get my hair cut!, pays an hour if it's a woman, I think, if it's a man it pays, he pays five hours, I think, of work he pays, five hours, I think, of work he pays. He's out of town, so the woman works by herself, she knows where the phone is. An' this new girl my mother 'as got was so upset, an' she didn't know any kind at work. She was brand new, an' she didn't know, she didn't even, . . .

This type of conversation contributed to Laura's being labeled schizophrenic (as well as retarded) once she was an adolescent.

Some of Laura's inappropriate responses to others' comments seemed to reflect difficulties with presupposition and implicature.

(10) [Re JB, L's older sister]

J: What kind of doctor is she going to be?

L: A female.

(11) [It is summer 1988. By now her sister has completed medical school and is a physician]

J: What kind of doctor is she?

L: A woman.

(12) [Talking about her sister's having gone to camp]

J: She went to Camp C on her vacation?

L: Yeah.

J: Oh.

S: By herself?

L: By bus.

For example, Laura's response in (12), however true, was inappropriate. Though she responded factually, she clearly missed the intent of the question. Shultz and Robillard (1980), in discussing the development of humor through intentional linguistic rule violation, might call this an example of "overliterality." Laura did not answer the actual question, seeming to attend more to the surface structural aspects of the previous utterance and less to its content.

In normal conversation such responses are often the stuff of jokes, where word play is used intentionally to create humor. In Laura's case, although her responses reflect her awareness of the semantic and structural ambiguities of certain utterances, she seemed unaware that such responses were in any way inappropriate or humorous.

The CYCLE analysis of discourse functions confirmed that although Laura was able to use some conversational conventions, she often did not do so consistently or appropriately. As stated in chapter 4, when Laura's performance was measured by the CYCLE-S, the majority of her errors were found to fall in the pragmatic as opposed to syntactic or semantic areas. Pragmatic analysis of data from normal children using the CYCLE-S methodology revealed that normal children generally use the full range of discourse categories (see appendix A) from an early age and have a very low error rate of 1.38%. Two samples of Laura's language were analyzed for pragmatic knowledge and her overall error rates were extremely high, 19% and 39%. Her error rate was high compared with that of normal children (under 2% for 3-year-olds). This is a significant finding. Laura failed to respond to questions and tended to introduce new topics inappropriately. In addition, she failed to grasp the implications of her interlocutor's utterances.

It is important to note that Laura grew up in a normal family environment and had the opportunity to learn language within a normal social context. However, from the very beginning Laura's social interactions were not always normal.

Laura's mother's diary indicates that poor social skills and abnormal pragmatics were evident from the earliest stages of Laura's development. On May 28, 1965, when Laura was 1¾ years old, her mother wrote, "She often goes off, seems quite unfocused and unfocusable—I feel sometimes with her as I did with H when she was 2 and 3 months; just don't know how to relate to her and help her relate to me. And it's very hard to chat away to her when she responds so little." By the time Laura could talk well enough to engage in conversation she was noted to talk incessantly about topics unrelated to the linguistic and social context.

In February 1969, when Laura was about 5½, her mother wrote that her "farthest behind area as I see it is social." She noted that Laura could "bounce the conversational ball back two or three times on nearly any subject, often on subjects we've already gone into together, often too in new areas where fresh thinking is taking place, often aloud in analogies." However, at this time she also observed a great deal of perseveration and stereotypy in Laura's speech.

In January 1970, when Laura was about 6½, her mother wrote, "The other thing I find *extremely* wearing is her talking. . . . We've been pleased at her language and concept development of course, and have encouraged her speech. But she talks—demanding replies *all the time*, often about the same subject, over and over."

It is clear from such entries and from comments in teachers' reports that Laura was not normal in her social interaction during her early years.

The range of knowledge that the child must acquire in order to use language appropriately in context is broad and complex. This learning begins at the prelinguistic level. The prelinguistic expression of needs, wants, .and intentions (Jaffe, Stern, and Perry 1973; Bruner 1975), early ritualized games (Gleason and Weintraub 1975; Garvey 1974), and action games are claimed to be some precursors to linguistic expressions of the same functions. Condon and Sander (1974) speak of linguistic-kinesic interaction as a source of language acquisition. In addition, interactive mother-child routines that begin during the prelinguistic stage are said to develop and become increasingly elaborated, resulting in the child's control over the structural aspects of language (Stern 1971).

Normal children seem to acquire pragmatic knowledge relatively early and quickly. It has been found that young children can and do adjust their language according to their audience, switching to simpler forms of discourse when speaking to younger children (Gleason

1973; Shatz and Gelman 1973) and using different registers depending on their partner's status or role (Ervin-Tripp 1977) or when talking to inanimate objects such as dolls (Sachs and Devin 1973). Preschool children are able to handle a wide range of grammatical features including modal auxiliaries, pronouns, and deictic terms (Shields 1978) and definite and indefinite articles (Maratsos 1976, 1979), features that are controlled at least partially by pragmatic factors.

According to Bates (1976), children's ability to distinguish old and new information is evident even at the one-word stage, when they are able to select the word that represents the most salient part of an idea (new information) in communicating their thoughts. Children also show knowledge of the rules of conversation, introducing, maintaining, and changing topics appropriately (Keenan 1974; Dore 1977). Bloom, Rocissano, and Hood (1976) observed turn-taking behavior at the two-morpheme utterance stage, noting that children at this stage did not maintain or elaborate on topics initiated by adults, whereas at the four-morpheme or 2-year-old stage children were able to do both. Toler and Bankson (1976) noted that the majority of responses given by 3-year-olds in their study were appropriate.

The implications of Laura's poor pragmatics are great, given the purported importance of pragmatics for language acquisition. Since she was able to learn and utter many structures and forms that she did not always use in a pragmatically appropriate manner, it seems unlikely that her grammar is built upon a pragmatic base. The fact is that although one may argue that many structures and forms have pragmatic functions, the acquisition of the structures and forms themselves cannot be *explained* by an appeal to pragmatics alone. Indeed, although Bruner (1975) feels that the emergence of language can best be described pragmatically, he acknowledges that the mechanisms involved in the elaboration of grammar out of a pragmatic base structure must still be defined.

As is evident from the above discussion, Laura's use of language as a communicative tool was extremely deficient. Although she could talk a great deal, her ability to converse and to use language effectively to convey a clear message was quite diminished. Diary and educational records indicate that these problems were evident throughout Laura's development. Laura's case thus argues against a linguistic theory that considers communicative functions to be the basis for structural and semantic aspects of language.

Chapter 6
Nonlinguistic Cognition

An examination of a broad range of Laura's nonlinguistic abilities gave me the opportunity to examine various claims about the relationship between language and cognition. Some researchers have assumed that the relationship between the two areas can be characterized in terms of a link between linguistic attainments and Piagetian cognitive stages (Sinclair (de Zwart) 1973, 1975b; Ingram 1975; Tremaine 1975). The classic concept of "stages" holds that there are clearly demarcated phases in child development, each of which is characterized by a "different kind of psychological structure" (Ginsburg and Opper 1969). However, there is some debate about whether the notion of "stage" is a useful heuristic (Brainerd 1978). It has been argued that a stage theory of development sets up artificial constructs and that cognitive development actually proceeds in a smoother, more slowly evolving fashion (Flavell 1978; Gardner 1983). As Flavell (1978, 187) writes, "Human cognitive growth may simply be too contingent, multiform, and heterogeneous—too variegated in developmental mechanism, routes, and rates—to be accurately characterizable by any stage of the Piagetian kind." Fischer (1978), though criticizing the specifics of Piaget's stage hypothesis, argues that the stage notion itself is a useful one that should be retained.

Others refrain from linking cognitive stages to linguistic stages, preferring instead to talk of the relationship of specific nonlinguistic skills to specific linguistic developments (for example, Ferreiro 1971).

Some claim that abilities across linguistic and nonlinguistic cognitive domains are reflections of a third, underlying general governing mechanism. In this framework general abilities putatively account for linguistic abilities like the capacity to see word class relationships, to concatenate elements, and to form complex linguistic structures. Abilities across domains are not simply analogous, but homologous—that is, derived from and governed by a common underlying mechanism. In this view nonlinguistic cognitive behaviors and linguistic abilities are not predicted to emerge in an invariant order. Individual differences as well as domain-specific factors contribute to the varying order in which abilities emerge across domains. However, it has been acknowledged that if two abilities are commonly governed, they should emerge within a relatively narrow time frame (Bates et al. 1977).

Correlational studies have provided the bulk of the data supporting the cognitivist position. A great deal of research has been devoted to linking both early and later linguistic attainments with cognitive attainments (Bates et al. 1977; Corrigan 1978; Bloom 1973; Nicolich 1977; Bates 1976; Beilin and Lust 1975; Ingram 1975, 1978; Beilin 1975; Tremaine 1975; Sinclair and Ferreiro 1970).

Some compelling work has centered around the search for "formal parallels" across domains. Studies have been done to illustrate that analogues to linguistic processes exist in other domains, the implication being that formal parallels constitute evidence for one underlying set of cognitive principles that manifest themselves in different domains. Investigators have compared language and action (constructive praxic activity) (Greenfield 1978; Goodson and Greenfield 1975), language and perception (Keil 1980), language and mathematical abilities (Pullman 1981), and language and gesture (Thal and Bates 1988; Thal, Bates, and Bellugi 1989).

In the following sections I detail Laura's performance in various nonlinguistic areas. Some abilities, such as those discussed in section 6.1, are associated with Piagetian theory. Others, such as handling of number concepts, hierarchical construction, and memory (sections 6.4, 6.8, and 7.2), are examined because they show a developmental progression. Some areas, such as classification, rule abduction, and hierarchical organization (sections 6.6, 6.7, and 6.8), are among those abilities researchers have assumed to reflect a common underlying governing mechanism. Certain abilities, such as drawing, copying, and constructional abilities, gave both cognitive and neuropsychological information. Neuropsychological and neurolinguistic results are primarily listed in chapter 7.

6.1   Piagetian Theory

The Piagetian structuralist or constructivist theory has provided a comprehensive framework for the study of the development of cognitive processes and has influenced theory and research in the fields of psychology, linguistics, and education. In both the original formulation of the theory and its various modifications, language is seen as one expression of more general cognitive capacities. The theory has retained ardent followers in spite of newer approaches to cognitive development that have arisen out of mathematics (such as category theory) and computer technology (such as information processing and artificial intelligence models). It has been suggested that alternative models of cognitive development can simply be incorporated into the general Piagetian framework, especially in view of Piaget's revisions of his own theory (Halford 1978; Beilin 1980).

Though far from perfect, Piaget's stage theory provides a useful framework for making some comparisons between Laura's abilities in the linguistic and nonlinguistic domains. Piaget specifies four invariant age-related developmental stages in his theory of cognitive development: the sensorimotor, preoperational, concrete operational, and formal operational stages. The first three stages and the abilities often associated with these stages are addressed here.

6.1.1 The Sensorimotor Stage

According to Piaget, the sensorimotor stage lasts from birth to about 2 years of age. Developments relevant to the subsequent emergence of language are said to occur in the latter portions of this stage. Whether these developments are seen as necessary and sufficient conditions, or simply necessary, depends upon the views of the particular researcher.

Sensorimotor interaction with the environment results in the acquisition of certain basic concepts, such as means-ends knowledge, the object concept, and semiotic functions, and it is these concepts that are considered by Piaget and his followers (for instance, Sinclair (de Zwart) 1971, 1973, 1975a,b) to be critical to subsequent cognitive developments such as language.

In stage 5 (12–18 months) of the sensorimotor period children are said to become innovative, exploratory, and adventuresome in their interaction with the environment, discovering new means to familiar ends. These emergent abilities have been described as the earliest, most primitive forms of problem solving. In addition, means-ends behavior is seen as possibly precursory to tool use, which in turn has been linked to language development (Bates 1979). Bates proposes that tool use and symbolic activity in children "involve some common structural capacities for part/whole analysis and substitution of parts within those wholes" (p. 322), "a capacity that must be shared with symbols in language and in play" (p. 331).

Children's evolving object concept is also said to reflect their emergent representational capacity. They can now conceptualize that an object has an existence and life outside their own and understand that the object can make a sequence of movements outside their perceptual awareness. The attainment of object permanence has been linked causally and chronologically to single word acquisition. Bloom (1973) claims that her child Allison did not begin to use words for objects in a stable, consistent manner until around 18 months, when object permanence usually emerges (according to traditional Piagetians).

Stage 6 (18–24 months) has been described as the transition to the next period of development in which the infant is able to use mental symbols and words to refer to absent objects. A crucial development of this stage is the emergence of the ability to mentally represent an absent object or action. The child is also said to develop the capacity to mentally differentiate between the symbol and its referent (the item or complex of items that the symbol stands for). This newly developed ability for representation is called the "semiotic function." The child is now capable of "deferred imitation"—in other words, of reenacting observed behaviors in detail at some later time. Another example of the semiotic function that emerges during this period is symbolic play. The child may hold a piece of bread crust in the air, make motor sounds, and say, "Airplane," or hold up a piece of clay and say, "Cookie." It is claimed that such abilities have obvious relevance to language since language involves the ability to represent and symbolize. In fact, some researchers claim that mental representation is the primary prerequisite for language (for example, Sinclair 1975b; Morehead and Morehead 1974). Others have observed that the onset of language acquisition correlates with the more dynamic aspect of sensorimotor intelligence such as means-ends behavior (Snyder 1975).

6.1.2   The Preoperational and Concrete Operational Stages

The preoperational stage roughly spans ages 2 to 6. Preoperational behavior is often defined as the absence of cognitive principles characteristic of the subsequent concrete operational stage, such as reversibility and decentration. There are, however, some definite developments characteristic of this period. The child is said to continue to develop abilities that emerged at the end of the sensorimotor period, namely, imitation, play, drawing, and mental imagery. Language acquisition is a significant achievement of this cognitive stage.

At the preoperational stage much of the child's reasoning is described as precausal, prelogical, and basically intuitive. With the onset of concrete operational intelligence between the ages of about 6 and 8, there is a marked transformation in the child's thinking. The child reasons in a qualitatively different, decidedly more mature fashion, at least from an adult's standpoint.

The subsequent concrete operational stage is said to span approximately ages 6 to 11. Whereas the preoperational child makes judgments on the basis of superficial perceptual phenomena, the concrete operational child uses mental operations to solve problems. Thus, if shown two equally long sticks that are then placed in a perceptually deceptive T configuration so that one looks longer, the concrete operational child can resist the perceptual trick and reason that the sticks are still of equal length.

Also, whereas the preoperational child has difficulty focusing on more than one feature of a problem at a time, a characteristic called *centration*, the concrete operational child is able to attend to numerous features simultaneously in problem solving, thus showing *decentration*. When water from a tall narrow glass is poured into a short wide glass, the operational child, able to attend to both the height and width of the glasses, can reason that the amount of water is unchanged.

In addition to possessing "spatial decentration," operational children demonstrate "temporal decentration" (Flavell 1977). Whereas the preoperational child has trouble focusing on anything but present states, the operational child is able to keep track of all past, present, and future states and the operations that produce them. She is able to mentally refer back to previous states and to project potential future states. Furthermore, the operational child's mental operations are "reversible." In other words, the child is able to mentally undo an operation (*inversion*) and is aware that certain factors in an operation can compensate for others (*compensation*).

6.1.2.1 Conservation and Seriation   Two abilities felt to be crucial indicators of concrete operational intelligence are *conservation* and *seriation*.

In conservation tasks, quantities are manipulated and the child must judge whether the manipulations or operations are relevant to the question at hand. Reversibility and decentration are purportedly required to make the correct judgments.

Seriation is the ability to systematically arrange a collection of items along a specific dimension such as size. Seriation requires reversibility, since one must be able to see the relationship of a given item to items on either side of it in the series. For example, an item is at once larger (longer, heavier, etc.) than some items in the series, and smaller than other items.

According to Piagetian scholars, certain linguistic structures also reflect the concrete operational features of reversibility and decentration. These nonlinguistic features are assumed either to be prerequisite to particular linguistic attainments (Ingram 1975) or to reflect common underlying mechanisms (Beilin 1975).

Decentration, for example, is purportedly evident in the child's ability to use coordination, in that the child is able to attend to several features simultaneously ("It's tall and it's thin"). Sinclair (1969) notes that in contrast, nonconservers tend to use undifferentiated terminology to describe materials differing in two dimensions. For example, if shown two pencils, one short and thick and the other long and thin, the nonconserver would describe both as "big," apparently attending only to the width of one and the length of the other.

Reversible operations are claimed to be reflected in the ability to use comparative and superlative constructions. Whereas nonconserving, preoperational level children use absolute terms to describe seriated items (the items are either "long" or "short," for example), conserving, operational level children are able to use comparative terminology. The feature of reversibility is evident in that these children, having identified the sticks from shortest to longest as "Short, longer, longer, longer . . . ," are then able to start with the longest stick and say, "Long, shorter, shorter, shorter . . . ," thus relabeling as "shorter" the sticks they have just previously called "longer."

Reversibility is also claimed to be evident in the child's use of temporal terms and concepts (Beilin 1975). Ferreiro and Sinclair (1971), for example, found that preoperational children are unable to reverse linguistically the sequence of two temporally ordered events. They observed that preoperational children had great difficulty when they were shown a sequence of actions involving two dolls and then were asked to describe the actions mentioning the second event first. The youngest children in the study (about 4½) either seemed to ignore the instructions, giving a description that retained the temporal order, or simply mentioned the two actions without any temporal indicators (for instance, "He went upstairs and she washed him"). Children of about 5½ attempted to use temporal indicators but also had difficulty with the task. During questioning, Ferreiro and Sinclair established that the children knew which event came first but simply could not encode or perform temporal reversals linguistically.

The attainment of concrete operational thinking has been considered prerequisite to the acquisition of many complex structures such as passives (Baldie 1976; Beilin 1975; Sinclair and Ferreiro 1970), cleft constructions, and productive nominalizations and other embedded constructions (Ingram 1975). Acknowledging that such linguistic structures often appear prior to the concrete operational period, Ingram (1975) hypothesized that although preoperational children may use such structures, they do not yet apply transformational rules. According to Ingram, complex sentences that the child produces at this stage are quite infrequent and are generated by a phrase structure grammar rather than transformationally (for instance, *I want to* + VP). In the concrete operational stage the child's grammar is hypothesized to undergo a major restructuring involving a shift from a phrase structure grammar to a transformational one. Restructuring or reorganization has been considered in various components of the grammar: for example, syntax (Brown, Cazden, and Bellugi 1968; Ingram 1975; Clark 1974, 1975; Bowerman 1982), morphology (Ervin 1964; Bloom, Lifter, and Hafitz 1980), and the lexicon (Bowerman 1974, 1982). However, the timing of this putative restructuring has not always coincided with the concrete operational phase. In studying complex sentences, Bowerman found evidence of restructuring already by age 3½, long before concrete operational intelligence is supposed to emerge. Parisi and Antinucci (1971) and Brown (1973) have also claimed that knowledge of transformational operations involved in embedding appears much earlier.

6.1.2.2 Classification Yet another indicator of concrete operational level intelligence is classification. Although the growth of classification abilities has been traced by Piaget and his colleagues from the preoperational and even sensorimotor periods on up, it is generally at the concrete operational level that these abilities are said to become fully developed.

Inhelder and Piaget argue that classification and seriation abilities originate in perceptual and sensorimotor structures, the most elementary cognitive structures, and although the development of these operations is independent of language, language may be dependent upon them.

According to Inhelder and Piaget (1964), early classificatory skills (stage I) seen in the preschool child (ages 2½–5) are nonhierarchical. Inhelder and Piaget refer to "graphic collections" by the young child (that is, the organization of materials in a syntagmatic fashion). Thus, if given a toy tree, man, flower, and woman, the child may group the man with the tree and the woman with the flower, saying, "The man is standing under the tree" and "The woman has a flower," instead of classifying the items according to shared attributes (plants, humans). Also, when given geometric shapes to classify, the very young child may make groups of identical formations—for instance, placing all the triangles atop all the squares to make a group of houses.

In contrast, the older child of 4 or 5 to about 7 seems to be able to classify on the basis of a given feature such as color, shape, or size—that is, paradigmatically—but has difficulty dealing with several features at a time. For example, the child at this age can make piles of squares and piles of red things but may have difficulty making piles of red squares.

The child with advanced classificatory abilities characteristic of the concrete operational stage is better able to deal with several classes simultaneously and to conceptualize subclasses as well as subordinate classes—in other words, to grasp hierarchical relationships. The child at this stage is thus able to deal with "class inclusion" whereby all members of one class are contained in another, but not vice versa. For instance, all roses are flowers, but all flowers are not roses.

6.1.3   Performance in Areas Associated with Piagetian Stages
See table 6.1 for a summary of Laura's performance on stage-related tasks.

Results of object permanence and means-ends testing. Laura succeeded on all tasks for object permanence and means-ends behavior (Uzgiris and Hunt 1975), indicating that she had attained stage 6 of the sensorimotor stage, knowledge considered by some to be prerequisite to language acquisition (Piaget 1980; Sinclair 1975b). Thus, Laura's cognitive level was not so low as to challenge the claim that sensorimotor achievements are at least necessary for the emergence of language.

It is likely that some awareness of the world and of objects and their properties is necessary for language development. However, there is already evidence from other sources that sensorimotor knowledge is neither sufficient nor even necessary for language acquisition. Goldin-Meadow, Seligman, and Gelman (1976) for example, note that although children may not produce object words until 1½ years of age, when object permanence is supposedly just developing, they comprehend object words much earlier developmentally. Huttenlocher (1974), too, reports that comprehension for object words can develop as early as 13–14 months.

Previous research has already demonstrated a temporal discrepancy between the emergence of mental representation and the emergence of syntactic representation, reflecting the lack of a causal or temporal link between the two abilities. Some children seem to acquire a degree of representation long before the emergence of syntax (Huttenlocher 1974; Corrigan 1978), whereas others begin combining words prior to demonstrating a representational capacity (Corrigan 1976; Ingram 1975, 1978). Studies of children learning American Sign Language as a native language also challenge the assumption that language development must wait for the attainment of sensorimotor knowledge. Multisign utterances have been observed as early as 10–12 months (Schlesinger and Meadow 1972; McIntire 1977), long before the time the putative cognitive prerequisites appear. Of course,

Table 6.1
Stage-related tasks

Area	Performance	Level
Classification	Can sort by color and shape; cannot do reversal shifting	Late preoperational
Classification/categorization	Cannot sort by gender, animacy, etc.	3-year level at best
Conservation	Does not conserve for length, solid or liquid quantity, weight, or number	Preoperational
Number Concepts	Lacks true counting concepts; can rote count	Preschool
Representational Abilities		
Drawing	Repetitive and perseverative; cephalopod humans	Preschool
Play	Little symbolic play noted; poor exploration of objects	Preschool
Sensorimotor Abilities	Shows object permanence and means-ends knowledge	Has attained Stage 6
Seriation	Cannot anticipate seriation; cannot seriate	Preoperational
Spatial Abilities		
Stereognosis	Stage IB-IIA	3½- to 4-year level
Copying	Stage IB-IIA	3½- to 4-year level

some would argue that object knowledge develops much earlier than has previously been assumed and that with improved, cleverer methodologies, all children will demonstrate object permanence prior to 12 months (Spelke 1982; Gelman and Gallistel 1978).

Results of conservation testing. Laura did not conserve for solid or liquid quantity, weight, or number. In a study by Uzgiris (1964), 85% to 90% of children over age 8:11 succeeded on similar tasks for solid continuous and discontinuous quantity. Wallach, Wall, and Anderson (1967) found that 55% of children conserved for liquid quantity by age 7:8.

Laura gave conserving responses on length tasks on two out of four occasions (in the second and third administrations). In the fourth administration care was taken to phrase the same/more test question so that the final clause of the question did not contain the conserving or correct response. This would rule out the possibility that echo responses would resemble conserving answers. On this occasion Laura, who was particularly alert and attentive, gave nonconserving responses to all questions. Lovell, Mitchell, and Everett (1962) found that by age 9, 67% of normal children who were given similar length tasks demonstrated conservation abilities.

Results of seriation testing. When given seriation tasks using rods of varying lengths, Laura was unable to draw a prediction of how the rods would look in seriate order and was unable to order the rods. Her most successful predictive drawing consisted of a series of parallel lines of roughly the same length and color. Laura's performance was thus at stage I, a preschool level.

Results of classification testing. Generally, when given circles and squares of different colors (red or blue) and sizes (large or small), Laura was not able to sort them spontaneously. She was able to sort by color when specifically asked to do so. However, she was not able to shift tasks and sort by size or shape even with repeated prompting. Kendler and Kendler (1962) found that preschoolers shifted tasks successfully. Inhelder and Piaget (1958) found that 56% of the 7-year-olds in their study were able to sort in at least two different ways (say, first by color, then by shape).

On one occasion Laura showed the ability to sort items along several dimensions. When presented with a set of colored shapes and asked to "Put them into groups; show me which ones belong together," Laura made four piles: red circles, blue circles, red squares, and blue squares (each pile containing both large and small shapes). Thus, although she ignored the feature of size, Laura showed the ability to deal with color and shape simultaneously.

In being able to sort colored shapes along two dimensions simultaneously, Laura was performing at a late preoperational, even early concrete operational stage. Sugarman (1981, 1982) found that using her methodology, children aged 24 to 36 months were also able to attend to two features in sorting tasks.

Results of class inclusion testing. Laura failed all class inclusion tasks, perhaps indicating that she had difficulty manipulating the hierarchical relationships among the classes and subclasses involved (for example, apples, oranges, fruit).

6.2 Representational Abilities

Insofar as language has been viewed as just one expression of a general representational capacity evident in other areas (Piaget 1951; Nicolich 1977), Laura's abilities in several semiotic areas were examined for comparative purposes.

These areas have also been researched from a non-Piagetian perspective. Kellogg (1970), for example, has described specific developmental features in children's drawing.

6.2.1 Play

Laura's interaction with objects was extremely deficient when compared with that of normal children. When shown an unfamiliar object, she demonstrated minimal interest in it and needed prompting and encouragement to explore it. Laura's lack of exploratory behavior with regard to objects in her environment may be linked to "cognitive motivation"[1] (Haywood and Wachs 1966; Haywood and Weaver 1967; Haywood 1971; Dobbs 1967).

Results of play observations. Laura seldom if ever engaged in make-believe play and did not particularly enjoy games or arts and crafts. She had no hobbies, although she loved to listen and dance to Beatles music. I observed symbolic play behavior on only one occasion. I had been trying to engage her in some dramatic play, using my red collapsible umbrella as a microphone with which to interview her. I was having little success in getting her to pretend, when suddenly she grabbed my umbrella and announced playfully that it was a tomato and that she was going to eat it. She pretended to bite the umbrella and then said she wasn't going to eat it after all. "Why not?" I asked. "Because it's not a tomato, it's an umbrella," she replied. Note that this is also a good example of sensorimotor level symbolic behavior.

A diary entry by Laura's mother written when Laura was 4:5 indicates that by that age Laura had shown representational abilities.

During a notable play period Laura reportedly transformed some clay from a "snake" to a "dead snake" to a "dead fish" to a "fish" to "cooking," as indicated by her verbalizations.

6.2.2 Drawing

Drawing gives insight into both representational and spatial abilities. Throughout the study Laura was occasionally asked to draw pictures. At times she was asked to draw something in particular, but generally she was encouraged to draw whatever she liked.

Results of drawing tasks. Laura's spontaneous drawings were quite perseverative and primitive. She almost always drew the same thing, a human consisting of head and legs, with eyes, nose, mouth, and sometimes hair (see figure 6.1). She also wrote her full name on most pictures. Laura frequently drew this stereotyped picture even when specifically asked to draw some other item. On one occasion with a great deal of prompting she drew her family. On another occasion she drew a quadrilateral shape and first called it a "motel," then a "McDonald's" (the American fast food chain), selecting words beginning with [m]. Normal children often label their spontaneous drawings representationally at age 2.

Another feature of Laura's drawing was that she liked to make sun-like shapes, a favorite gestalt of young children according to Kellogg (1970). Such "suns" are not necessarily representations of the solar sun but are simply a stage of drawing common in preschoolers. After drawing the sun-like shape in figure 6.2, Laura initially said it was a dog, then called it a sun. Often humans drawn by children at this stage have rays emanating from them. Indeed, Laura's humans sometimes featured such rays (see figure 6.3). Kellogg states that sun gestalts usually do not appear until after humans, but they are already common at ages 3 and 4.

Laura sometimes drew objects that she had apparently been taught to draw in formulaic fashion. For example, one day I asked, "Laura, will you draw me a picture?" She responded, "Of a turkey?" and drew a turkey by tracing her hand (see figure 6.4).

Laura's drawings were at the preschool level at best. In addition to being developmentally delayed, they were perseverative and stereotypic.

6.3 Spatial Abilities

A copying task and a stereognosis task gave some idea of Laura's spatial concepts and their relation to her performance in other cognitive areas.

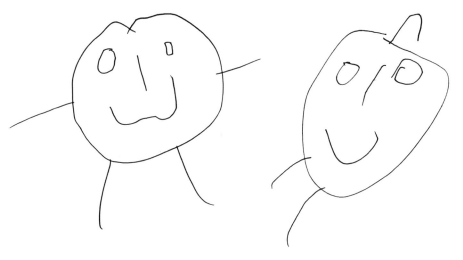

Figure 6.1
Two drawings by Laura of human figures

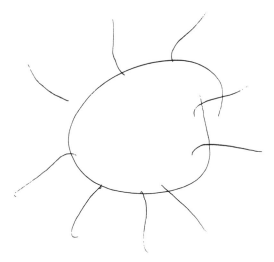

Figure 6.2
A drawing by Laura of a sun-like shape

Figure 6.3
A drawing by Laura of a human figure with rays emanating from it

Figure 6.4
A drawing by Laura of a turkey (made by tracing her hand)

Results of spatial abilities testing. On the Piaget and Inhelder (1967) copying tasks Laura performed at the IB-IIA stage, roughly the 3½- to 4-year-old level. At this stage in copying, curved lines begin to be distinguished from straight-sided lines but the square and triangle are still indistinguishable.

On the Stereognosis test (Laurendeau and Pinard 1970) Laura did fairly well on part I, which involves palpation of familiar objects. She scored 6 out of 11 when asked to name the object palpated and 11 out of 11 when asked to point to pictures of the items palpated. On part II, involving palpation of topographical shapes, she scored 6 out of 12 when asked to point to a picture of each shape palpated and 4 out of 12 when asked to point to a duplicate shape in an array. On part III, involving palpation of Euclidean shapes, she scored 4 out of 12 when asked to point to a picture of each shape palpated and 5 out of 12 when asked to point to a duplicate shape.

This performance is again at the IB-IIA stage, or the 3½- to 4-year-old level. Laura's performance on these two tests additionally reflects that she was functioning at a preschool level in spatial tasks.

6.4   Number Concepts

Since the acquisition of number concepts show a definite, age-related (stage-linked) developmental progression, this was another important cognitive area to examine. Also, since certain number concepts and operations are considered to be specialized to the left hemisphere like language (see, for example, Gardner 1976), it was of interest to explore how Laura's number concepts compared to her linguistic level.

Results of number testing. Laura had some awareness of number. She could discriminate small sets, for instance 2 versus 3, when given Gelman's "Magic Show" task. She correctly pointed to all numbers except 4 and 9 when asked to point to selected printed numbers from 0 to 9.

Although she could recite numbers into the teens, her true counting and numerical concepts were poor. I observed her "count" up to seven items, pointing to each item in the array. However, she often made errors, even when the array contained only three or four items. Laura generally knew that she had to point to each item, but she might assign two numbers to a given item and might count the same item several times. Thus, she failed to demonstrate knowledge of the one-to-one principle in counting (Gelman and Gallistel 1978). In those cases where she had correctly counted the items in an array, she could not then immediately say how many items there were. She thus failed to show an understanding of the cardinal principle. Her counting skills, then, were merely rote-learned.

In addition, Laura could not tell time and had no concept of money values. Unlike many 2- or 3-year-old children, she did not know her own age, although her guesses were usually reasonably close to her actual age. Laura's mother noted her daughter's difficulty in this area when she was 6: "When I ask her 'How old are you?' she has never yet told me 'six' without prompting—she'll say 'three' or 'two.'"

Laura's responses to infinity questions further highlight her limited understanding of number concepts. When asked one day to name the biggest number she could, she said, "Three." When asked to add one to that, she said, "Eight." On another occasion the biggest number she could name was "Ten." When asked to add one to that, she said, "Two"; and when asked to add another one, she said, "Three."

Laura demonstrated similar difficulty in dealing with numbers in everyday situations. Whenever she was asked to give a staff member in her residential setting a particular number of pennies (say, five), Laura would invariably err in counting, giving too few or too many.

Laura's number concepts were at a preschool level at best.

6.5   Logical Sequencing

To understand or construct a sentence describing ordered events, the normal individual appears to require knowledge of the logical structure underlying the sentence. That is, although conceptual awareness of the temporal relationship of a series of events is reflected linguistically in the use of temporal adverbials, tense/aspect forms, and the like, this does not show the extent to which linguistic aspects that overtly mark temporal and sequential concepts are tied to the concepts themselves. A similar question was posed with regard to classification. In both cases it is important to determine to what degree the distinctions we make linguistically are simply a mirror of those we make conceptually. This question was explored by asking Laura to put pictures into logical order as described in appendix B.

A child's ability to organize pictures into a logical sequence may also reflect "event knowledge," a term used in conjunction with schema theory (Rice 1984). Schemas have been defined by Mandler (1979) as "set[s] of (usually unconscious) expectations about what things look like and the order in which they occur" and by Rice as mental structures "whose elements are related to one another on the basis of spatial or temporal continguities instead of class membership and similarity relationships." Even young children have an awareness of familiar sequences of events: for example, 3-year-olds are able to describe (Nelson, quoted in Rice 1984) and act out (Garvey 1977) reasonably accurate sequences of events.

Results of logical sequencing testing. Laura was unable to order pictures into logical sequences, an ability reflected in normal 5-year-olds (Friedman 1978; Curtiss and Yamada, unpub. data).

Indeed, as her memory performance indicates (see section 7.2), Laura sometimes had difficulty recalling sequences of events in their correct order. In contrast, as described in chapter 4, she made extensive use of temporal terms in her speech, inserting them into appropriate places in the sentence in spite of her limited conceptual understanding of some of the forms.

6.6   Classification/Categorization

In addition to providing information about her cognitive stage, Laura's classification abilities were valuable in view of the claim that classes and categories play a significant role in the formation of semantic and syntactic categories (Inhelder and Piaget 1964). We classify and categorize our world both linguistically and nonlinguistically. The ability to classify things in action (that is, to use a category of objects for the same action) is said to be reflected in language as the ability to formulate linguistic categories, such as NP and VP.

To compare her linguistic and nonlinguistic ability to classify along a given dimension, Laura was given additional tests of concepts that are coded in language. For example, I compared her ability to mark gender in language (that is, in pronominal forms) with her ability to do a nonlinguistic sorting task where gender and animacy were the crucial distinguishing features.

Results of classification/categorization testing. When given a set of cards depicting either males or females and asked to "Make two piles of things that are the same or that go together," Laura did not sort on the basis of gender. (It should be noted that Laura had the concept of sameness.) Similarly, she did not sort on the basis of human versus nonhuman features when given a stack of cards depicting either people or animals. Since Laura was able to distinguish men and women from one another in everyday life, her difficulty with these tasks did not seem to reflect a lack of conceptual knowledge of the categories involved, but rather a failure to abduce, on the basis of available data, the task or rule at hand. This is a very low level of performance since work with normal children has revealed that even 3-year-olds are able to do the same gender-based sorting task that Laura failed (Curtiss and Yamada, personal observation).

Laura's difficulties on classification tasks that required her to sort similar items are intriguing, since in language she was able to categorize elements on the basis of similar features. Her ability to plug various adverbial forms into appropriate places in a sentence indicates that she perceived that adverbs form a class and can be interchanged. Similarly, she was able to sort linguistic elements appropriately into noun and verb classes. She did not make form/class errors.

6.7 Rule Abduction

Other abilities hypothesized to inhere in lingustic and nonlinguistic domains are general-purpose inductive strategies (Reber 1973; Dore 1975; de Villiers 1980; Maratsos and Chalkley 1980; Sinclair 1975b).

Results of rule abduction testing. On the Rule/Nonrule Governed Learning subtest of the Muma Assessment Program (Muma and Muma 1979) Laura failed to demonstrate rule-governed learning even after 50 trials. On the Simple Rule Acquisition test Laura failed to reach criterion (10 consecutive correct answers) on test 1, and testing was terminated. On another day I decided to test beyond the criteria for failure to see whether she would ever learn the rule. When given tests 2, 3, and 4 consecutively, she gave 10 consecutive correct answers only after 50 trials, on the last 10 items of test 4. This was her best performance. When given the four Simple Rule Acquisition subtests on a subsequent occasion and tested far beyond the criteria for failure, she failed to abduce the rule even after 80 trials.

Laura's performance on the Simple Rule Acquisition test was poorer than that of any of 10 normal preschoolers whose performance was compared with hers. Five of the 10 children aged 3 to 5 abduced the rule within or after the first 10 items of the first test. Two of the children, one 3:0 and one 4:3, learned the rule after 3 items. Four additional children abduced the rule on the second test within the first 10 items. One child, 5:5, abduced the rule afer 1 item on test 2 and another child, aged 5:2, abduced it after 3 items. Thus, 9 of 10 children rather quickly abduced the rules, requiring from 3 to 30 trials to learn them.

6.8 Hierarchical Construction

The presence of hierarchical structure in various cognitive domains has been hypothesized to reflect homology, or shared cognitive principles (Piaget 1980; Bates 1979; Greenfield and Schneider 1977). Classificatory skills exhibit hierarchical structure. Greenfield and her colleagues have also examined hierarchical organization in the action (constructive-praxic) domain. Greenfield and Schneider note that "studies of children's three dimensional constructions reveal increasing hierarchical complexity with age (Goodson and Greenfield 1975) as do studies of language development." In both domains children deal with individual elements before combining and building hierarchically organized, more complex structures. The ability to formulate complex linguistic structures and complex hierarchically organized concrete structures (for instance, with blocks) is argued to reflect a general hierarchical capacity. Greenfield and Schneider claim that the existence of "formal" parallels in action and language are an indication that a unitary of cognitive principles underlies both language and nonlanguage domains.

Goodson and Greenfield (1975) and Greenfield and Schneider (1977) explored the role of three structural principles in complex combinatorial activity—hierarchical complexity, interruption, and role change—claiming that both the process of construction and the completed structure itself reveal commonalities between action and language. They note that just as children form simple sentences before combining them into hierarchically more complex structures, so do they first manipulate individual items like blocks before combining them in hierarchically complex configurations.

They also note that the use of complex structures can be linked to an increasing capacity to deal with interruptedness. In construction play the child can build one part of the structure, go to another part, then return to complete the first part. Whereas very young children avoid interrupted strategies in construction play, as they grow older, their tendency and capacity to use and deal with interruptedness increases (Goodson and Greenfield 1975).

In language, as well, children seem to develop an increasing capacity to deal with interruptedness and complex structures (Bever 1970; Slobin 1971). In order to understand and produce a sentence containing a center-embedded relative clause, for example, the child must hold one part of the sentence in abeyance and then return to it, in order to successfully complete the sentence: *The girl / who hates parties / left.*

Finally, role change is evident across domains. Linguistically it is apparent in certain relative constructions where the coreferential NP plays a different grammatical and semantic role in the main clause than in the embedded clause. Nonlinguistically it is apparent in manipulative play, where a cup can function as an active moving element, then be put down and used as a receptacle, that is, as a passive object/locus element.

Results of hierarchical construction testing. Laura was very poor at constructing hierarchical models of sticks and blocks. When copying models of stick configurations, she could not even copy a simple three-stick bridge, and when copying block models, she could not construct anything more complex than a simple three-block bridge. Laura seemed aware that she should use more blocks for the more complex models but could not recreate the hierarchical relationships involved. Children of 2:9 and 2:10 in Vereecken's study (1961) were able to construct a simple bridge.

Thus, whereas Laura was producing hierarchically complex linguistic structures, she was not able to construct anything but the simplest structures in the visuoconstructive domain.

6.9   Discussion

In view of Laura's performance on the above cognitive tasks it is significant that she was able to produce such a range of linguistically complex constructions. Cognitivists would predict that Laura, lacking reversibility and decentration for example, would not be able to use the linguistic structures that purportedly rest on such cognitive attainments.

Sinclair (1975b, 225) claims that production and comprehension of structures in which the clause order and temporal order are noncongruent should be impossible without concrete operational level thought: "*The girl goes upstairs when the boy has parked the car. . . .* It remains to be shown that retarded children in their early teens with a mental age of below six are incapable of understanding and constructing such sentences although this would seem plausible." Laura's performance provides the crucial clinical evidence. Contrary to Sinclair's predictions, Laura used a variety of structures that have been linked to reversibility and decentration, such as passives (1), comparatives (2), embedded structures (3), and complex constructions where the order of the clauses is not congruent with the temporal order of the actions (4).

(1) [Re barracudas]

   I was never swallowed by one.

(2) [Talking about a dress she wore to a wedding]

   I got skinnier and skinnier an' it fit.

(3) I'm very good friends of a girl that cuts (. . .)'s hair, that I'm working with.

(4) . . . I told the police when I got lost.

When viewed alongside her linguistic abilities, Laura's nonlinguistic performance provides compelling evidence against both the Cognitive Hypothesis and the Correlational Hypothesis.

The strong form of the Cognitive Hypothesis states that cognition is sufficient to account for language development except in cases of severe language deprivation or of sensory or motor deficits (Miller 1981). It predicts a close correlation between language and cognitive development. Laura's performance argues against this hypothesis, given that her language level exceeds her cognitive level.

The weak form of the Cognitive Hypothesis states the cognition is necessary but not sufficient to account for language acquisition. Cromer (1974b, 1976a, 1981) has discussed this version of the Cognitive Hypothesis extensively, proposing that although cognitive achievements may be integral to language learning, it may be necessary to posit certain specifically linguistic capabilities. This hypothesis predicts that language will keep pace with cognitive development or will lag behind it. However, it does not predict a profile of selectively enhanced language. Laura's performance refutes this view as well. Although testing indicated that she lacks the cognitive abilities of reversibility and decentration, her grammar includes linguistic structures assumed to require these notions. Passives, comparatives, and embedded structures are very much a part of her productive grammar.

Some researchers have hypothesized that nonlinguistic abilities may not be prerequisite to language per se; rather, both nonlinguistic and linguistic developments may be behavioral expressions of some other underlying governing mechanism or mechanisms (Bates 1979), a view sometimes called the Correlational Hypothesis. An indication of this would be the discovery of general cognitive principles across domains.

Whereas the Cognitive Hypothesis predicts that abilities will emerge in an invariant order, with nonlinguistic cognitive attainments preceding or coinciding with language attainments, the Correlational Hypothesis predicts that the order of emergence may vary, while still maintaining the primacy of general cognitive functions over linguistic ones. Correlationalists account for the varying order of emergent abilities by invoking the concept of "blockage," whereby a given ability is judged to be absent for superficial peripheral reasons rather than for lack of the underlying cognitive mechanism itself. Such a theory predicts the possibility of the enhanced language profile, since the cognitive deficiencies could be explained away by peripherally based difficulties like apraxia or emotional disorder. If no such source of blockage exists, some slight variance in order of emergence is still permissible, since domain-particular factors are assumed to affect the emergence and expression of a given general ability. However, as stated earlier, advocates of this view acknowledge that abilities across domains should appear within a reasonable time of one another (Bates et al. 1977).

Evidence of common denominators in behaviors across domains is felt to reflect common organizing principles across domains. Some abilities believed to exist across domains are categorization and classification (Rosch et al. 1976), rule abduction or extraction (or hypothesis generation) (Osherson and Wasow 1976; Neimark 1970; Maratsos and Chalkley 1980; Cromer 1976a,b), and hierarchical organization (Greenfield 1978). These abilities may themselves be manifestations of general, underlying, more basic abilities and are not mutually exclusive; for example, categorization and rule abduction may both require the more basic capacity to extract regularities.

One could argue that Laura's capacity to classify items and abduce rules in the nonlinguistic domain is relevant to her capacity to do so in language. Recall that Laura was able to sort on the basis of color and shape (although she could not then shift tasks and sort along another dimension). Does the fact that she finally (after 50 trials!) abduced a simple "same" rule on one occasion indiate that she had adequate rule-abduction capacity to account for language? Similarly, does the fact that she was able to sort on the basis of two features simultaneously mean that she had enough classificatory ability to acquire language? The nonlinguistic rules Laura learned were extremely simple, and hardly seem comparable to the linguistic rules and constraints she was able to master.

Of course, poor performance on specific tasks may not reflect lack of the relevant ability. For example, the type of rule abduction tested in the nonlinguistic domain may have simply failed to capture the relevant or critical parameters of the hypothesized general rule-abduction capacity. Also, it is perhaps unfair to compare Laura's rule-abduction abiltiy on a time-constrained task with her apparent ability to apprehend linguistic rules, since she had the opportunity to learn rules in the latter domain over a more protracted period. Nonetheless, the nature of the linguistic rules she had acquired seems qualitatively different from the nonlinguistic rules for which she was tested.

Why wasn't Laura given nonlinguistic rule-abduction tasks that were more analogous to linguistic rules? First, given Laura's great difficulty with the simple nonlinguistic tasks just reviewed, tasks of any greater complexity seemed out of the question. Second, there are few if any nonlinguistic rule-learning tasks that are truly comparable to linguistic rule learning.

Not everyone agrees with this viewpoint. Maratsos and Chalkley (1980) propose that the learning of syntactic categories is similar to learning in other domains—for example, to concept formation (Nelson 1974; Rosch et al. 1976) and the learning of social roles. They point out that a social role such as *mother* is defined not by its inherent characteristics but more by how it functions in relation to other parts of a system. They claim that what goes on in acquiring this knowledge is similar to what goes on in the learning of syntactic categories. What children must learn about the "systematicity and abstractness" of the linguistic system, along with its "arbitrary exceptions, idiosyncrasies, semigeneralizations," and so on, parallels what they must learn about "characteristically human activity." As Yourcenar (1961) puts it,

> Grammar, with its mixture of logical rule and arbitrary usage, proposes to a young mind a foretaste of what will be offered to him later on by law and ethics, those sciences of human conduct, and by all the systems wherein man has codified his instinctive experience. (cited in Maratsos and Chalkley 1980)

However, in implying that the principles involved in the learning of syntax also underlie these other knowledge systems, Maratsos and Chalkley do not explain why the principles are expressed in the different domains at such different times in the child's development. Although children are talking fluently by age 4, for example, the complexities of government bureaucracy are still far beyond them. Similarly, although Laura had definitely acquired much syntactic and morphological knowledge, she had little understanding of governmental structure.

    (5) J: Who's the president of the United States?

         L: Lincoln.

Neimark (1970) implies a similarity between learning rules for "constructing a grammatical utterance" and for "being a good child." It is difficult to believe that this is the best example of a nonlinguistic parallel to linguistic rule abduction. We are hard pressed to find a system comparable to language because no other system is so simultaneously tied up with conceptual, perceptual, and social factors. Pinker (1979) argues that positing some kind of theorem for rule generation is theoretically not defensible, since if children were simply gifted with some general rule-abduction capacity, the time required to test data and form the correct hypotheses about language would be indeterminable. Thus, the range of possible grammars seems to be constrained, most likely innately so. From an empirical as well as a theoretical standpoint, then, the principles governing language and those governing nonlinguistic cognitive domains are better described as distinct from one another, although there is probably some overlap.

In Laura's performance the hierarchical features of complexity, in-terruptedness, and role change were evident in language but not in the action domain. Piagetian scholars might attribute this to "decal-age," the notion of uneven performance that has been built into the theory. The idea that linguistic and nonlinguistic abilities are linked by common underlying principles predicts that the order in which behaviors emerge may vary. However, some constraints should be placed upon this notion. Variation in order of emergence can occur, but both linguistic and nonlinguistic behaviors are expected to de-velop within a reasonably narrow time frame. Laura was in late ad-olescence by the time this study took place and had not yet acquired the relevant nonlinguistic behaviors. Her performance clearly calls into question the idea that the nonlinguistic behaviors tested are ho-mologous with linguistic abilities acquired more than 10 years earlier.

6.10   Summary

In general, Laura's performance on nonlinguistic tasks was poor. In most areas such as copying, drawing, seriation, and number con-cepts, she performed at about the 3-year-old level. In many areas she performed at a 3½- to 4-year-old level. In Piagetian terms she was generally functioning at a preoperational level.

Laura also did not do well on nonlinguistic tasks that have been considered to reflect common organizing principles, such as catego-rization, rule abduction, and hierarchical organization. Given that she was nearing the end of adolescence at the time of this study, it is doubtful that the relevant abilities will ever emerge.

Chapter 7
Neuropsychological Testing

It is now believed that each hemisphere of the brain is specialized to process information in particular and distinct modes—in other words, that the hemispheres are distinguished by their strategies of processing rather than simply by the functions they mediate. Whereas the left hemisphere is thought to process in a sequential, analytic, linguistic mode, the right is believed to process in a parallel, holistic, spatial, and nonlinguistic mode (Witelson 1977).

Laura was given neuropsychological tests to see whether she would show strength on tasks associated with one or the other hemisphere.

Laura's performance on many tasks is summarized in table 7.1.

7.1 The Boston Diagnostic Aphasia Examination

On the basis of the BDAE subtests given to Laura, a rating scale profile of speech characteristics was prepared for her. With scores closer to 7 in melodic line, phrase length, articulatory agility, and grammatical form, and closer to 1 (that is, below 4) on paraphasias in running speech, word finding, and auditory comprehension, Laura's profile was similar to that of a Wernicke's aphasic.

7.2 Memory

Memory clearly plays an integral role in learning and cognitive processing and was therefore a crucial area to examine in relation to language acquisition. It is not, of course, a unitary phenomenon; several different types of memory (such as short-term, long-term, immediate, auditory, visual, sequential, and spatial) have been posited.

Memory has been linked to intelligence, showing a clear developmental progression (Hagen, Jongeward, and Kail 1975; Terman 1916), and indeed has long been used as a measure of intelligence. It is not

Table 7.1
Neuropsychological tasks

Task	Performance (score)	Level (comments)
Disembedding		
Preschool Embedded Figures Test	2	Below mean of 8.8 for 2¾-year-olds
Southern California Figure-Ground Perception Test	7	Below mean for 4.0- to 4.5-year-olds
Environmental Sounds Recognition	20	Of 25 (80%); No norms
Facial Recognition	15	Defective performance
Familiar Voices Recognition	4	Of 5 (80%); No norms
Gestalt Perception		
Mooney Faces	17	Of 40 (42.5%)
Perceptual Integration Test		Does not demonstrate part-whole integration
Memory		
Auditory		
Auditory Memory Span Test	6	Below the level of adequacy; rating −2
Auditory Sequential Memory (ITPA)	8	Psycholinguistic age 3:0
Visual		
Corsi Blocks	No norms	Can do only one-tap items consistently; some two-tap items
Knox Cubes	0	
Memory for Designs	28	Off bottom of scale
Visual Sequential Memory (ITPA)	9	Psycholinguistic age 4:1

yet clear just how memory is related to language, although some investigators have found a correlation between auditory sequential memory and language (Graham 1968; Masland and Case 1968; Menyuk 1964).

There is also neurological evidence linking auditory short-term memory and language; the left cerebral hemisphere, considered the language hemisphere in normal right-handers, has been found to be better at auditory sequential short-term memory (Warrington and Weiskrantz 1973; Zaidel and Sperry 1974; Milner and Teuber 1968). Bloom and Lahey (1978) point out, however, that the correlation between auditory memory span and language does not necessarily indicate a causal or dependency relationship between the two areas, noting that 3-year-olds who can only repeat lists of two or three unrelated words are nonetheless able to understand and produce rather long sentences, perhaps because of the facilitative effects of semantic structures. In contrast, autistic children often have superior short-term memory skills alongside poor linguistic abilities.

Results of memory testing. Despite the neurological evidence indicating that auditory short-term memory and language may both be lateralized to the left hemisphere (in the normal right-hander), Laura's case indicates that they are dissociable, even in development.

Laura did very poorly on word and digit span tests. On Wepman and Morency's Auditory Memory Span Test, a word span test, she could not repeat sequences of more than three items, obtaining a score of 6 ("below the level of adequacy"). On the Auditory Sequential Memory subtest of the ITPA, a digit span test, she could not repeat sequences of more than three numbers, earning a score of 8 (psycholinguistic age score 3:0). She performed similarly on a nonstandardized word span test that I designed, consisting of some of her favorite words (for instance, *Beatles, cake, fat*).

Laura's performance on the Memory for Auditory Nonverbal Stimuli (MANS) developed by Curtiss, Kempler, and Yamada (unpub.) was even worse than her word and digit span performance. Although Laura was able to associate each of three familiar sounds with the appropriate pictures, she could not do even two-item sequences. This performance is equivalent to that of only the very youngest children in the normative sample thus far tested (2- to 3-year-olds). In addition, on the Verbal Mediation test, given to determine whether Laura would make use of rhyming to aid memory, she recalled 27% of type 1 test cards (rhyming) as compared to 13% of type 2 (unrelated) and 0% of type 3 (conceptually related). Thus, Laura apparently made use of the phonemic similarity of the cue words associated with type 1 cards.

Laura did very poorly on the Knox Cubes test, giving only perseverative responses to each stimulus item, tapping blocks 1-2-3-4 each time a sequence of two or more taps was modeled. She also did very poorly on the Corsi Blocks test, imitating only one- and two-tap sequences.

On the Visual Sequential Memory test of the ITPA Laura was able to reproduce sequences of up to three tiles, attaining an age score of 4:1. She was able to do some but not all three-tile items. Thus, her visual and auditory sequential memory performances were similar.

Laura's memory span correlated with her IQ level. Miller (1956) found that normal subjects could process 7 ± 2 chunks of information, compared to 4 ± 1 for retarded individuals.

Laura showed the same discrepancy between memory for sequences of unrelated words and memory for sentences that Bloom and Lahey (1978) observed in normal 3-year-olds. Laura's ability to repeat sentences containing up to nine morphemes and her ability to understand simple sentences both seem to indicate that she made use of semantic and syntactic structure to aid memory.

In natural contexts Laura had great difficulty remembering even the simplest factual information. For example, she did not know coin values. One day, when we were buying an apple from a vending machine, I put four coins of differing values in my palm, held them out, and said, "Take the quarter." Laura took the penny. She also had difficulty with rote counting, days of the week, months of the year, and the like—items that teachers (including her mother) attempted to teach her many times.

In contrast, Laura often showed the ability to remember events. For example, upon being told that a friend was getting married, Laura remembered this information and months later was even able to recall the name of the prospective spouse.

A week after she stayed overnight at my home I questioned her to find out how much of the visit she remembered. She seemed to recall the entire experience—what we'd done, what we'd eaten at each meal, and so on. However, when talking of a past event she would at times conflate several experiences, confusing people, places, and actions. Sometimes she mingled a remote event with a more recent one and referred to both as though they had just occurred.

In addition, Laura had difficulty remembering where she was supposed to be at given times even though her school and living schedules were very regular. On several occasions it was necessary for Laura to show me where she was supposed to go after our session—for example, to occupational therapy or cooking class. However, she usually showed no awareness of where she needed to go next, simply standing and staring blankly despite my pleas for her to tell or show me.

The distinction between semantic and episodic memory made by Tulving (1972) captures to some extent the difference between the types of things Laura did and did not remember. Semantic memory holds facts (for instance, chemical formulae, rules for addition and multiplication, the knowledge that autumn follows summer). Episodic memory holds temporally coded information and events, ". . . information about how things appeared and when they occurred" (Klatsky 1975). Semantic memory is not as malleable and transient as episodic memory. Because there is a constant influx of new information, material in episodic memory easily becomes irretrievable. It appears that Laura had poor semantic memory and relatively better episodic memory.

Laura's confusion about series of past events and about her daily schedule (which also involves a sequence of events) reflects her difficulty with semantic memory. Memory for individual events is more gestaltic and episodic than memory for a sequence of events, which requires an attention to ordering that is more akin to the rule-like quality of semantic memory.

There is one glaring inconsistency in characterizing Laura's memory ability in terms of episodic and semantic memory components. Although she was supposedly poor in semantic memory, she was able to learn the rules of language, considered by Tulving to be part of the domain of semantic memory.

7.3   Dichotic Listening

Dichotic listening is used as an experimental technique to reflect cerebral lateralization. Generally the task involves presentation of two simultaneous, competing stimuli, one to each ear. Each ear is connected to the brain by two auditory pathways: the ipsilateral or same-side connection and the contralateral or opposite-side connection.

In dichotic listening the ear contralateral to the hemisphere lateralized for a particular function performs better than the ipsilateral ear. Normal right-handed adults show a slight right ear advantage when verbal stimuli are presented (left hemisphere processing) and a slight left ear advantage when nonverbal stimuli are presented (right hemisphere processing) (Curtiss 1977; Kimura 1967).

Results of dichotic listening testing. Laura had a great deal of difficulty on the dichotic listening task. The method described in appendix B was chosen because it required no reading, only pointing responses in a free visual field. On the first 30 training pairs, in which identical stimuli are presented to each ear, Laura scored 13 correct. She got all [ti] and [di] items correct (5 each) and 3 [gi] items. In spite of this poor pretest performance, two blocks of 60 dichotic pairs were presented to "see what would happen."

Laura did quite poorly on both blocks. However, with regard to error rate and ear advantage, her performance in both cases was remarkably consistent. In the first block of 60 she missed 33. Of the 27 correct responses, 16 were right ear items and 11 were left ear items. In the second block of 60 she missed 34. Of the 26 correct responses, 16 were right ear items and 10 were left ear items. In both cases she showed a slight right ear advantage, suggesting left hemisphere dominance for language processing.

7.4   Abilities Possibly Controlled by the Left Hemisphere

7.4.1   Short-Term Memory, Sequencing, Numbers

The left hemisphere is hypothesized to process information sequentially and analytically, and the right hemisphere is thought to operate in more parallel and holistic modes. Some investigators propose that the left hemisphere is not a "language hemisphere" per se but rather a "sequencing hemisphere." Krashen (1972) suggests that oral language, a sequential phenomenon, is lateralized to the left hemisphere.

Since these hypotheses posit a strong correlation between sequencing ability and language, it is provocative that Laura did so poorly on sequencing tests.

As discussed in section 7.2 Laura's performance on both auditory and visual short-term memory tasks was poor. She was unable to hold sequences of more than three items in memory, and sometimes she could not repeat even three-item spans. She also had great difficulty in carrying out sequences of actions. When involved in a task requiring several steps, she had to be prompted each step of the way. In addition, she found numbers and counting very difficult. After years of education she still could not count even five items consistently.

7.4.2   Disembedding

In disembedding tasks the individual must locate a simple figure that is contained and hidden in a larger, more complex figure. Whether this is a left or right hemisphere ability has been a matter of debate, since it correlates strongly with aphasia (Teuber and Weinstein 1956; Russo and Vignolo 1967). However, evidence indicates that when the embedded item is familiar or simple, the right hemisphere can perform the task (Curtiss 1979; D. Zaidel, personal communication), possibly because of that hemisphere's strategy of template matching (E. Zaidel, as cited in Curtiss 1979). Such tasks were also appropriate because disembedding or figure-ground perception has been claimed to be involved in receptive language (Irwin 1948; Oakland and Williams 1971; Townsend and Bever 1977).

Results of disembedding testing. On the Preschool Embedded Figures Test Laura did very poorly, obtaining a score of 2, quite a bit below the mean of 8.81 for 2:9-year-olds (Waldrop, as cited in Coates 1972). On the Southern California Figure-Ground Perception Test (Ayres 1972) Laura obtained a score of 7, below the mean of 9.5 for 4:0- to 4:5-year-olds, the youngest children in the normal sample.

7.5   Abilities Possibly Controlled by the Right Hemisphere

7.5.1   Gestalt Perception (and Part-Whole Perception)

Clinical data indicate that gestalt perception and part-whole perception (which actually seems to be a type of gestalt perception) are right hemisphere abilities in the adult (Newcombe 1969; Lansdell 1968; Nebes 1971). These abilities involve conceptualizing a whole upon exposure to only a part or parts. In part-whole tasks the stimulus is a single, identifiable part (a piece of pie) and the whole (the entire pie) must be conceptualized from this single part. In gestalt tests the whole must be conceptualized from an apparently disparate set of parts. For example, a partially obliterated silhouette is shown and the subject must identify the whole silhouetted item.

Results of gestalt perception testing. On the Perceptual Integration Test Laura's responses reflect that she attended either to the parts or to the wholes rather than to both simultaneously. Elkind, Koegler, and Go (1964) found that 5- and 6-year-olds tend to see only wholes or parts (centration), 7- to 8-year-olds see both parts and wholes but do not integrate them, and older children (8- to 9-year-olds) are able to see wholes and parts in relations to one another ("It's a man made out of fruit"), evidencing part-whole integration. Of the 9-year-olds in the study, 76% showed this ability (compare with Prather and Bacon 1986, however).

Laura did very poorly on the Visual Closure subtest of the ITPA, obtaining a raw score of 3 for an age score of 2:2.

On the Mooney Faces test Laura obtained a score of 17 out of 40 (42.5%) with much prompting. On each item she had to be reminded of the six possible categories, and much encouragement was needed to get her to respond. Because of the slow, laborious fashion in which Laura carried out this task, two sessions were needed to administer it. Many of her responses seemed to be guesses.

7.5.2   Facial Recognition
The Test of Facial Recognition (Benton et al. 1975) is a standardized procedure for assessing the ability to identify and discriminate photographs of unfamiliar faces. Benton et al. found a link between right hemisphere impairment and defective performance on this test, a result supported by the findings of De Renzi and Spinnler (1966) and Warrington and James (1967). There are two versions of this test: a long (54-item) version and a short (27-item) version from which a long version score can be projected.

Results of facial recognition testing. Laura was given the short version of the test and scored 15 (projected long version score = 32), a "defective" performance.

7.5.3   Enviromental Sounds Recognition
Although research examining right hemisphere dominance has generally used visual stimuli, some studies have investigated whether the right hemisphere is also the primary processor for certain auditory stimuli such as familiar phrases (D. Van Lancker, personal communication; Van Lancker and Kempler 1987), environmental sounds (Carmon and Nachshon 1973; Curry 1967, 1968), and certain types of music (Kimura 1967; Gordon 1970; Cook 1973).

Results of environmental sounds recognition testing. Although she did only half of Van Lancker's 50-item Environmental Sounds Recognition Test, Laura was able to correctly identify 20 of the 25 items. Laura's performance was almost identical to that of my son Aaron, who was about 23 months old at the time of testing.

7.5.4   Familiar Voices Recognition
Speech is generally associated with left hemisphere processing. However, the right hemisphere may be the primary processor for particular aspects of speech such as overall intonation contours (Blumstein and Cooper 1974) and emotional tone (Heilman, Scholes, and Watson 1973; Searleman 1977). According to D. Van Lancker (personal communication), familiar voices recognition may rely on right hemisphere gestaltic perception, analogous to the recognition of familiar faces. One indication of this is the facility with which most people can recognize the voices of relatives, friends, acquaintances, colleagues, and media personalities. In a recent study Van Lancker,

Kreiman, and Cummings (1989) found that deficits in recognizing familiar voices were significantly correlated with right hemisphere damage.

Results of familiar voices recognition testing. Laura was given the familiar voices recognition task twice. On her better performance she identified four of five voices. The one voice she failed to recognize was my own, the voice least familiar to her of the five. The other voices on the audiotape were those of immediate family members and a family friend, all people she had known since birth or early childhood.

7.6   Abilities Possibly Controlled by Both Hemispheres

Insofar as the Graham and Kendall Memory for Designs test and the Benton Visual Retention Test require a sequence and variety of behaviors (attending to and visualizing a pattern, and reproducing this pattern through a complex sequence of motor movements), they are felt to involve both hemispheres. Laura performed at abysmal levels on both tests.

On the Memory for Designs test her score was 28 (the highest possible score being 0), a score so poor that it was off the bottom of the scale.

On the copying version of the Visual Retention Test, which is designed to test visual perception, visual memory, and visuoconstructive abilities, Laura did very poorly, attaining a score of 0. Frequently she drew undifferentiated circular shapes in response to the various models and ignored the peripheral shapes completely. Sometimes in response to test stimuli she drew faces and had to be constantly reminded to try to draw the stimulus figures.

7.7   Summary of Performance on Neuropsychological Tests

Although Laura excelled at language, an ability localized to the left hemisphere in most people (Krashen 1972; Dimond 1980; Geschwind 1974; Springer and Deutsch 1981), she showed no similar ability in any other area believed to be controlled by that hemisphere. (See table 7.1 for a summary of Laura's performance on neuropsychological tasks.) On short-term memory, sequencing, and computational tasks, for example, Laura did extremely poorly. This suggests that her island of abilities was a small, specialized one indeed, an island of linguistic abilities.

Although the trend in recent years has been to describe the left hemisphere as an analytic, sequencing hemisphere rather than as a language hemisphere per se, Laura's performance indicates that it is possible to dissociate certain kinds of sequencing abilities from linguistic abilities. Sequencing, then, at least the kind tested here, does not seem to be as closely linked to language as has been previously assumed.

Laura's relatively poor performance on part-whole and gestalt perception tests contrasts with her facile performance on the Auditory Closure test of the ITPA. Whereas Laura was not able to project the whole from looking at a part in the nonlinguistic domain, she seemingly found the task easy in the linguistic domain. Of course, it is possible that the distinction in her performance was due to modality factors, with her better skill being in the auditory as opposed to visual modality.

Laura was able to do a few of the tasks thought to be governed by the right hemisphere, such as familiar voices recognition and an experimental version of an environmental sounds recognition test (Van Lancker, unpub.). Van Lancker has hypothesized that this test taps right hemisphere abilities.

In natural settings I noted that Laura could do simple jigsaw puzzles, a visuospatial ability presumably governed by the right hemisphere. One of Laura's teachers told me that Laura could solve two 12-piece puzzles simultaneously, with the pieces of both puzzles mixed together. However, Laura's performance on many other visuospatial right hemisphere tests was quite poor.

Laura differed from previous subjects in that in her case no other cognitive ability was spared along with language. Previous studies seemed to discover at least one intact ability that correlates with language, most notably auditory short-term memory. These data have been said to support the hypothesis that whereas semantics is tied to conceptual development, syntax is more bound to processing abilities like short-term memory and sequencing abilities (Menyuk 1964; but compare Cromer 1976a and Bloom and Lahey 1978). Laura's case refutes this view.

Unlike what has been found with other hyperlinguistic subjects, Laura's auditory memory span did not correlate with her syntactic level. Whereas she had difficulty remembering three-item sequences, she produced sentences up to 20 words in length. Her short-term memory for sentences seemed appreciably better than her memory for unrelated items; she could repeat sentences up to nine morphemes in length. Structure seemed to aid memory performance rather than vice versa.

Laura's memory correlated more with her IQ than with her linguis-· tic level. Although auditory memory and language may both be lateralized to the left hemisphere in the normal right-hander, Laura's performance suggests that these abilities and dissociable.

Generally, language stood alone as Laura's cognitive strength; no other ability strongly correlated with it.

Chapter 8
Discussion

J: How many nights did you stay there? [*At a hotel with her family*]
L: Oh, about 4 out of 1.

As the preceding chapters illustrate, Laura's linguistic abilities out-stripped her nonlinguistic abilities. Her achievement was not that she attained linguistic sophistication in the complete absence of cognitive ability, but rather that she did so with a much *diminished* cognitive capacity. This case would be infinitely less provocative if Laura could be described as a mindless loop system that takes in input and spews it back out unanalyzed. In fact, certain severely autistic children, par-rots, and mynah birds seem to function in this fashion, echoing words, phrases, and sentences they have heard, without any under-standing of their structure or meaning.

Laura did not simply echo. Though her speech was sometimes dif-ficult to interpret because of false starts, unintelligible phrases, and neologisms, her errors and her ability to create novel forms attest to the productive nature of her language.

As such, this case poses some strong challenges for certain theories of the relationship between language and cognition, specifically those that argue for the primacy of cognition over language:

> Language and cognition can be clearly separated only in one sense; intellectual development is possible without language, but language acquisition is bound to the elaboration of cognitive structures in general. (Sinclair 1975b, p 225)

Laura's selectively intact language profile counters claims that ad-vanced linguistic attainments rest upon nonlinguistic attainments. She used many linguistic structures that purportedly depend upon Piagetian concrete operational abilities such as reversibility and de-centration, but she failed the hypothesized prerequisite concrete op-erational level tasks. Her performance shows that many nonlinguistic abilities are neither sufficient nor necessary for the emergence and development of grammar.

Laura's performance profile also challenges claims that abilities across cognitive domains are manifestations of a third, underlying general governing mechanism. Laura acquired language many years before this study, yet she had still not acquired many nonlinguistic abilities. A gap of over 10 years between the emergence of abilities in one domain and the emergence of abilities in another presumably indicates that they are not commonly governed.

Significantly, Laura did poorly on various nonlinguistic tasks that purportedly reflect general underlying cognitive principles, such as classification, hierarchical construction, and rule abduction. Whereas she was very deficient at building hierarchical structures in the non-linguistic domain, she could construct complex hierarchical structures linguistically. Of course, discovery of hierarchical structure across domains does not in itself imply shared governing mechanisms, since hierarchical organization can be found in most complex systems of the universe (Curtiss, Yamada, and Fromkin 1979; Fromkin and Klima 1984).

If similarities across domains are to have any significance, they must be more specialized in nature than those that have been proposed up to this point. The kinds of constraints evident in one domain should also be evident in others. Thus far, however, convincing analogies at this level have not been discovered. Some investigators seem to assume that the use of similar terminology in two domains constitutes sufficient evidence that analogy (or homology) truly exists (Curtiss, Yamada, and Fromkin 1979).

Inherent differences in constraints upon say, the physical as opposed to the linguistic domain are immediately evident. Limitations in the visuoconstructive domain are very much linked to physical laws. For example, a hierarchically complex block structure must be fairly symmetrical in height in order to stand. Such purely physical considerations clearly do not constrain embedded structures in language.

Another problem with specifying formal parallels is that cross-linguistic and cross-cultural factors have not been taken into account. For example, children's use of subject-verb-object word order has been likened to early object manipulation. However, children acquiring language do not universally adhere to this order.

If formal parallels do in fact exist, they have yet to be identified. Pinker (1979) states, "The algorithm that we need does not exist." To date, mathematical and computer-based research has shown that inductive capacities in a given domain must be innately and uniquely adapted to that domain and that constraints upon the system must operate for learning to occur (Pinker 1979; Wexler and Culicover 1980).

As Chomsky (1980, 245–246) puts it, "There seems little reason to suppose that the principles of grammar or universal grammar have any close analogue in other systems, though naturally one must keep an open mind about the matter."

Laura distinguished herself from previous hyperlinguistic subjects in that in her case no other cognitive ability was spared along with language. Previous studies have often found at least one ability that correlated with language, most notably, auditory short-term memory.

In some characterizations, aspects of language are considered to be linked to other aspects of cognition in differing ways and to differing degrees. Whereas semantics is assumed to be tied to conceptual development, syntax is assumed to be tied to processing factors like short-term memory and sequencing. The information-processing approach, for instance, assumes that perceptual, attentional, and memorial processes play a crucial role in taking in and transforming information: "Learning . . . can be viewed as the process of adding to or modifying the human memory system" (Klatsky 1975, 4). By this account, difficulties or deficiencies in short-term memory should result in syntactic deficiencies.

It is notable, then, that Laura had a poor memory span yet relatively good syntactic abilities. Clearly, syntactic capacity involves something more than just memory span capacity. Perhaps semantics contributed to Laura's capacity to remember sentences, or perhaps her knowledge of the structural aspects of sentences (aside from the semantic) facilitated her memory. She seemed to know where to put various types of structural elements even though she did not always fully grasp their meaning.

Laura's data are also relevant to the continuing debate regarding the relationship between syntax and lexical semantics and the roles these areas play in language acquisition (see for instance, Grimshaw 1981; Pinker 1984, 1987, 1989; Landau and Gleitman 1985). For example, do children learning language use the semantics of individual words (acquired from observation) to predict the syntax (semantic bootstrapping) or do they use knowledge of syntax to learn about individual word meaning (syntactic bootstrapping)? Both positions assume links or connections between the two domains. The question is, where does the language learner begin? Data from individuals like Laura cannot resolve the issue, but can be instructive. We should clearly proceed with caution before assuming that mastery of one domain accounts for acquisition of the other.

Not all areas of Laura's language were uniformly advanced. Laura seemed to have a special talent for acquiring syntactic knowledge. Whereas her speech was structurally rich and complex, its content was much less sophisticated and sometimes anomalous. These data challenge both the notion that language acquisition consists primarily of learning how to express linguistically what one already knows nonlinguistically (Schlesinger 1971; Slobin 1973; Nelson 1974) and the notion that language learning is simply a mapping of form onto meaning (Bloom 1970; Bowerman 1973a,b; Brown 1973; Schlesinger 1971, 1974). Laura's profile challenges the conceptualization of grammar as semantically based and the notion that syntax depends upon semantics.

To some extent, Laura's semantic knowledge more accurately reflected her general conceptual limitations. However, her performance also indicates that semantic knowledge is not simply a mirror of conceptual knowledge and vice versa. The two domains are separable. Laura seemed to have a special talent for acquiring lexical items that she did not necessarily fully understand. For example, her difficulties with time and numbers resulted in many amusing utterances. Despite her lack of understanding of many terms, she enjoyed using them in appropriate positions in her speech. This discrepancy in the learning of form and content occurs transiently in normal development. Bornstein (1985) reports that there is a stage in normal development where color naming is "unsystematic and unstable," and many investigators have observed a stage in which children either use one term for all colors or use several color words haphazardly. An individual who does not know which color word goes with which color does not necessarily lack color concepts. Nonlinguistic testing may reveal color discrimination abilities but a failure to associate nonverbal color concepts with the appropriate linguistic terms. For example, Cook (1931) found that younger children could match colors more accurately than they could name them.

The inability to match words with concepts is distinct from the lack of conceptual and/or perceptual awareness per se. Of course, even a perceptual deficit does not necessarily prevent an individual from learning certain linguistic terms. Helen Keller was able to write vivid poetry using color words even though her blindness precluded a clear understanding of color.

It was evident that Laura could perceive numerical differences to some degree and that she had some very general notions of these concepts. She could discriminate sets of two or three items, indicating that she could differentiate them perceptually. However, her number concepts were limited and her ability to consistently associate number terms with their correct referents was poor. Apparently, a conceptual deficit affects the manner in which a form is used but does not preclude the learning of the form itself. In describing her parent's large home as having three rooms, for example, Laura did not have to understand "threeness" before being able to acquire and use the word *three*, albeit erroneously.

That cognition is not equivalent to semantics is further exemplified by cross-linguistic variability in semantic categorization. For example, both the English-speaking child and the Japanese-speaking child likely perceive the same conceptual/perceptual distinction between "singularity" and "plurality," but this knowledge is not marked identically in both languages. English-speaking children must learn that plurality of objects is often marked on the noun that refers to them, whereas Japanese-speaking children need not mark the conceptual distinction in this way. Similarly, Japanese-speaking children, but not English-speaking children must learn to use different suffixes depending on what class of nouns they are counting (long, narrow objects, animate objects, and so on). Thus, although there may be universal constraints on concept formation (Rosch 1978; Rosch et al. 1976), there are many ways to divide up the world linguistically. Different languages do so in different ways, and each child must learn his or her own language's distinctions. Accounting for conceptual development does not predict or determine how a given language will divide up the world semantically, nor does it explain how or why we have the capacity to do so.

Laura's performance also challenges claims that pragmatic factors play a primary role in the acquisition process and that social and communicative functions are the basis for language structures and features (Givón 1979; Bates and MacWhinney 1979, 1982). The sentiment that interaction with the environment crucially affects and shapes language development is also found in social-interactive approaches to language acquisition (Snow 1972, 1977; Snow and Ferguson 1977; Dore 1974; Bruner 1974, 1975; Ochs and Schieffelin 1979; Zukow, Reilly, and Greenfield 1979). Although her pragmatic functions were extremely impoverished, Laura used syntactic structures such as relatives and passives that some claim to be functionally motivated by pragmatic factors (listener's perspective, new and old information, and the like).

Early in language acquisition the child probably makes use of pragmatic information when and wherever possible. However, such information seems to facilitate acquisition of communicative skills rather than grammatical knowledge. Cromer (1981) argues that although the focus on social-interactive factors has increased our knowledge of aspects of communication, it has failed to elucidate the processes responsible for the acquisition of linguistic *structure*. Research shows that mothers do not seem to "tune their syntactic complexity to the growing language competence of their children through this crucial age of syntax acquisition, the period from one to two and a half years" (Newport, Gleitman, and Gleitman 1977, 123–124), indicating that Motherese functions to teach communicative but not necessarily structural knowledge.

Givón (1979) and Bates and MacWhinney (1978) admit that a completely transparent form-function relationship does not always exist in language. Because of language change, some forms are synchronically abstract, with no apparent functional motivation. Although certain formal characteristics may be traceable in some way to functional origins, such functional motivations do not account for how or why a given child is able to learn the rules of language. Still to be accounted for is the child's capacity to acquire opaque forms, that is, forms whose histories are unavailable to the language learner. Purely functionally based grammars may be relevant to accounting for certain language changes, but not for how language is acquired.

The behavioral and cognitive evidence is that Laura possessed an island of linguistic ability. Could this island be characterized along hemispheric parameters? For example, were Laura's left hemisphere functions relatively more intact that her right hemisphere functions? Neuropsychological testing showed that her left hemisphere abilities as a group were not uniformly enhanced. In fact, language was the only putatively left hemisphere ability that was at all remarkable.

In certain respects Laura's behavior was reminiscent of individuals with right hemisphere damage. For example, Laura's language exhibited a clear discrepancy between structure and function, the former being much more enhanced than the latter. This gap was also reflected in her ideational versus her affective awareness. For example, her capacity to know when she should feel sad seemed relatively better than her capacity to feel the emotion itself. Similarly, individuals with right hemisphere damage sometimes exhibit the capacity to show intellectual but not emotional awareness (E. Zaidel, personal communication).

So far it has not been possible to identify which part of Laura's brain is disturbed and exactly how it is disturbed. "Hard" neurological evidence of what is going on in Laura's brain has been difficult to come by. Attempts to do NMR testing, for example, have been unsuccessful (Laura was unable to lie still enough for one test). Tachistoscopic results and auditory evoked potentials were also impossible to obtain because of Laura's cognitive limitations and her difficulty in the testing situation.

For the time being we must be content with the behavioral description of Laura as mentally retarded with unknown etiology. Various clinicians and teachers have also called her autistic, schizophrenic, and a savant. However one wants to label her, there is no doubt that she has the relatively rare profile of selectively intact language alongside depressed cognition. Significantly, this high language–low cognition profile was observed from Laura's earliest developmental stages on into adolescence. Other types of subjects who are now being investigated show this profile at older ages but not necessarily during early childhood. For example, some older Williams syndrome children (ages 10–16) show a relatively better linguistic than nonlinguistic performance whereas this profile is not always found in the younger children being studied (Thal, Bates, and Bellugi 1989). The Williams syndrome subjects also seem to have less of a semantic deficit, leading one to suspect that their profile reflects a specific visuospatial disability rather than generalized retardation. Further research with these and similar individuals is clearly in order.

There are many views regarding the nature of language learning and the relationship between language and other mental abilities. Most of the approaches do not constitute true theories of acquisition, but rather descriptions—and partial descriptions at that. The well-known Indian metaphor of a group of blind men attempting to describe an elephant, however overused, aptly captures the current situation. Each individual, groping and feeling a different part of the large creature, concludes that he has achieved an understanding of the animal. Each is partly correct but, having explored only a portion of the whole, fails to gain full knowledge of the entity being studied. Likewise, the different perspectives on language acquisition are all correct to some extent, but many, having focused only upon selected aspects of the metaphorical "elephant," fail to explain and understand the whole. In surveying formal models of language learning, Pinker (1979) alludes to this state of affairs. Stating six conditions that a theory of language acquisition should meet, he notes that "no current theory of language learning satisfies or even addresses itself to all six conditions" (p. 218).[1] Even Pinker's list seems a bit incomplete: it lacks the condition that a theory of language acquisition should posit mechanisms consistent with what we know about neurology and biology.

Theory must at some point be linked to biology. As Marshall (1980, 106) puts it, "We have so far failed to construct functional process models (psychological theories) that can mediate between noun phrases and neurons." Perhaps we are a breath closer to this goal with the discovery of populations like Turner's syndrome and Williams syndrome individuals, where there are indications that certain profiles of ability can be linked to factors at the genetic level. Notably, current results in biology support a shift away from purely functionally based conceptions of language and cognition. Molecular biology is supplying more and more evidence that change is not governed by function. As Piatelli-Palmarini (1987) puts it, nature is by nature nonparsimonious. Many structures, mechanisms, traits, and innate dispositions exist "for no reason at all":

> Selection acting on a vast, profligate and highly articulated repertoire of innate structures proves to be the most productive explanatory hypothesis, not only at the level of differential rates of survival of cells inside a given organism, but even at the level of the mind, in the growth of language and knowledge. (Piatelli-Palmarini 1987, 200)

A particularly relevant issue is innateness. Is language part of our biological or genetic imperative? In the nativist or innatist position the child is not viewed as an empty organism who faces the language acquisition task with the proverbial blank slate, but rather is assumed to be equipped with an innate complex of abilities specifically designed to learn language (Chomsky 1975, 1980; Roeper 1982). This innate knowledge is claimed to provide clues to what constitutes a possible natural language and to direct children to consider only a very limited class of grammars as they set out to acquire language. Evidence for this innate capacity is the fact that normal children readily acquire language within an astonishingly brief period, internalizing a finite set of rules with which to produce an infinite set of well-formed utterances.

Can the development of language be ascribed to some sort of "language organ"?

> It might be proposed that various "mental organs" develop in specific ways, each in accordance with the genetic program, much as bodily organs develop; and that multipurpose learning strategies are not more likely to exist than general principles of "growth of organs" that account for the shape, structure, and function of the kidney, the heart, the visual system, and so forth . . . . Rather, specific subcomponents of the genetic program, coming into operation as the organism matures, determine the specific properties of these systems." (Chomsky 1980, 245)

Recent theoretical developments in evolutionary biology indicate that structures, mechanisms, and innate dispositions cannot necessarily be described in terms of an adaptational framework. We now see a crucial shift in assumptions, where external constraints are assigned a very peripheral role (Piatelli-Palmarini 1987). How does a child know so much without being explicitly taught? Learning by association and analogy simply does not account for the speed and facility with which most children, including mentally retarded ones, acquire language.

The enhanced language profile is predicted only by models that consider aspects of language to be autonomous from other cognitive systems. Such a profile is not predicted by models that are purely cognitively, semantically, or pragmatically based. Likewise, the performance of idiots savants and prodigies can be accounted for only by a theory positing that human knowledge comprises interacting but independent systems (see, for example, Gardner 1983).

The data in this study support the recent trend toward an integrated model of language acquisition, one that involves numerous cognitive systems, the social-interactive environment, and perception, but also posits innate, language-unique factors. Whereas data from adult aphasics and Alzheimer's disease victims indicate that once established, language can continue to function in spite of selective deficits (Whitaker 1976), Laura's case shows that language can *develop* without the full support of other cognitive systems.

Syntax emerged most unscathed by Laura's nonlinguistic deficits, indicating that it is relatively more independent of nonlinguistic cognition than other aspects of language. Since social-interactive factors and internal factors like general cognition apparently cannot account for our capacity to learn the rules of grammar, innate, language-unique cognitive principles may be involved (Fromkin and Klima 1984; Osherson and Wasow 1976; Cromer 1981; Roeper 1978, 1981, 1982). For example, the knowledge of grammatical categories like *noun* and *verb* and the ability to learn and/or perceive such grammatical notions as *subject, direct object,* and *indirect object* seem to be uniquely linguistic. (Fromkin and Klima point out that certain features of phonological systems also appear to be unexplained by human production/perception capacities.)

By contrast, semantics is less independent. However, it is not a singular entity. Some aspects of semantics are linked more to structure; others are tied more to conceptual ability. Modular conceptualizations of language aptly capture the distinction. For example, Chomsky's theoretical model describes language as consisting of the computational and the conceptual components. The conceptual component interacts closely with other aspects of cognition, and the computational component includes the rules of language and is autonomous. The areas traditionally defined as semantics exist in both the computational and conceptual components. Whereas semantic rules are considered part of the computational component, the learning of particular lexical items and their meanings is considered part of the conceptual component. Laura's profile might well be described as a dissociation between the computational and conceptual components of language.

Semantics may also involve uniquely linguistic classificatory abilities. Laura's language reflected her special talent for sorting out lexical items semantically and for using them in syntactically appropriate locations. Because of her semantic knowledge, she was able to give semantically related responses to questions and comments. However, her conceptual deficiencies often resulted in nonfactual answers. Thus, her language also showed a dissociation of semantic and conceptual knowledge.

Positing the existence of a highly evolved cognitive system that includes uniquely linguistic features is not an ad hoc notion. There is already evidence that humans have other biological adaptations whose function is specifically linguistic. For example, it is now evident that the human vocal tract has evolved in such a way that it differs markedly from that of nonhuman primates (Lieberman 1972). The modifications and differences seem to have evolved primarily so that a wider range of speech sounds could be produced.

Nonlinguistic social, conceptual, perceptual, and processing factors all undoubtedly contribute to language acquisition. However, as clinical and theoretical evidence indicate, such factors cannot provide a complete account of language acquisition.

By purportedly showing that cognitive and linguistic developments are linked, cognitivists further assume that explanations for nonlinguistic development likewise account for language. However, as has been pointed out elsewhere (Bowerman 1978; Cromer 1976a, 1981; Pinker 1979; Wanner and Gleitman 1982), accounting for conceptual and social-interactive development does not automatically account for language-learning mechanisms. There is still the problem of explaining how or why children discover the formal devices to express linguistically what they may already know nonlinguistically. For example, accounting for conceptual development fails to elucidate how or why children develop increasingly more complex ways of expressing those concepts linguistically. In addition, it fails to account for children's capacity and propensity to learn formal linguistic features and structures (such as particle shift) that do not seem functionally or semantically motivated.

Laura's case is an important addition to the small list of studies that give evidence for the dissociation of language from other cognitive abilities. Her performance provides crucial empirical support for a model of language that acknowledges the multidimensional aspects of language. Aspects of language are tied to nonlinguistic systems by tethers of differing lengths, and some are perhaps untethered, enjoying an independent status. The data presented here strongly indicate that any viable account of language acquisition must incorporate the notion that language is at least in part governed by principles that are unique to it.

Appendix A
Description of Some Linguistic Measures

A.1   Comprehension: Receptive Language Measures

A.1.1   CYCLE-R

The receptive battery was developed to obtain detailed information about a subject's linguistic knowledge in the areas of syntax, morphology, semantics, and phonology.

The battery consists of four subbatteries; syntax, morphology, semantics, and phonology. Each contains a wide range of tests that permit the tracking of development in each grammatical component.

Although it is impossible to completely separate linguistic ability from test-taking ability in formal receptive language tasks, CYCLE tasks are simple in order to minimize task demands as much as possible. Pictures are clear and simple. In addition, the CYCLE-R controls for chance in numerous ways (for example, with adequately large arrays, carefully chosen decoys or foils, and repetition). To administer most CYCLE-R subtests, the examiner reads a test sentence aloud and asks the subject to act out or follow the instruction, or to point to the picture corresponding to the test sentence.

A.1.2   Token Test

Ten or 20 small plastic chips ("tokens") are presented to the subject in a predetermined array. The tokens vary in color (red, white, blue, green, yellow), size (large and small), and shape (circles and squares).

The test given to Laura consists of six parts. Instructions increase systematically in length from part to part, with the instructions in part F increasing in structural complexity as well.

Part A: Show me a square.

Part B: Show me the blue circle.

Part C: Show me the large green square.

Part D: Take the white square and the green circle.

Part E: Take the small blue circle and the large yellow square.

Part F: If there is a black circle, pick up the red square.

A.2   Production: Expressive Language Measures

A.2.1   CYCLE-E

Items on the CYCLE-E involve a sentence-completion format. Two-picture arrays are common. Pointing to the top picture, the examiner describes or refers to that picture. The examiner then points to the bottom picture and starts a sentence that the child must complete. For example, "(pointing to the top picture) Here is a dog, and . . . (pointing to the bottom picture) here are two ____." Single-picture arrays also appear in this test. For example, the examiner points to a picture of an unhappy-looking boy sitting at a table with a woman standing next to him. The examiner says, "Brian's mother said, 'Please drink your milk, Brian.' But Brian said, 'No, I ____'" (Ans: *won't*).

A.2.2   CYCLE-S

Three separate spontaneous speech analyses from the CYCLE-S were performed: grammatical, semantic, and conversational.

A.2.2.1   Grammatical Analysis   The grammatical analysis consists of giving one of five weighted scores (1–5) to a prescribed set of syntactic and morphological structures (see table A.1) in a given language sample.

1 = Obligatory but omitted

2 = Semantically/pragmatically inappropriate *and* syntactically ill formed

3 = Semantically/pragmatically appropriate *but* syntactically ill formed

4 = Semantically/pragmatically inappropriate *but* syntactically well formed

5 = Correct response. Semantically/pragmatically appropriate *and* syntactically well formed

Thus, for each element being analyzed, a score of 2 to 5 is assigned to each occurrence of that element. (Thus, if the element being analyzed is subject pronouns, a score of 2 to 5 is assigned to each occurrence of a subject pronoun.) Obligatory but omitted instances are also tallied and assigned a score of 1. Then the scores are summed and a

Table A.1
CYCLE-S: Grammatical analysis categories

Noun phrases	Auxiliary
Determiners/Demonstratives	Regular Past Tense
Quantifiers	Irregular Past Tense
Subject Pronouns	Tense Assignment
Object Pronouns	Regular Past Participles
Reflexive Pronouns	Irregular Past Participles
Indefinites	*Have* (Aux)
Relative Pronouns	Present Progressive: *be*
Dummy *it/there*	Present Progressive: *-ing*
Possessive Morpheme *-s*	Uncontracted Modals
Regular Plurals	Contracted Modals
Irregular Plurals	*Verb Phrases*
Locative Prepositions	Verbs
Case-Marking Prepositions	Verbs with Particles
NP Present in PP	Predicate Adjectives/Nominatives
Operations	Third Person Subject Pronouns
Subject-Aux Inversion	Non–Third Person Pronouns
Subject Questioning	*Be* (Verb)
Object Questioning	Other Equational Verbs
Other WH Movement	*Be* Contraction
Do Support in Questions	*Other*
Negative Placement	Subordinating Conjunctions
Do Support in Negatives	Coordinating Conjunctions
Negative Contraction	Infinitival Complements/Same Subject
Ellipsis/Deletion	Infinitival Complements/Different Subject
You Deletion	Infinitival Complementizers
Particle Movement	Other Complements
Preposed Indirect Object	Adverbials
Subject Relativization	Active Voice Word Order
Object Relativization	Simple Declaratives
Relative-*be* Deletion	Comparative *-er*
Equi-NP Deletion	Superlative *-est*
Other Subordinate Clauses	Passive: *be*
Some → any	Passive: *get*
Passive	Passive: *-en*
	Passive with Agent

mean is computed. The closer the score is to 5, the more frequently the subject uses the feature correctly.

A.2.2.2   Semantic Analysis   A sample of the subject's language is assessed for use of a specified number of semantic functions and categories. As with the grammatical analysis, the subject's use of each function or category is tallied according to weighted scores.

1 = Obligatory but omitted
2 = Semantically inappropriate
3 = Correct; semantically appropriate

A.2.2.3   Conversational (Pragmatic) Analysis   A sample of the subject's language is assessed for use of a specified set of discourse functions (see table A.2). Mean weighted scores are given to each occurrence (or obligatory but omitted instance) of a given discourse function. The weighted scores are:

1 = Subject does not do where appropriate
2 = Subject does inappropriately
3 = Correct; subject does appropriately

The conversational analysis also produces a ranged score, equal to the total number of different discourse functions used by the subject.

A.2.3   Developmental Sentence Scoring
In the developmental Sentence Scoring assessment (Lee 1974; Lee and Canter 1971) 50 consecutive, nonecholalic, "complete" sentences are evaluated in terms of eight grammatical features (where "complete" means "includes subject and verb"). Each scorable item is given a score from 1 to 8, with higher scores reflecting develop-

Table A.2
CYCLE-S: Conversational analysis categories

Takes turns	Interrupts at appropriate points
Establishes new topic	Labels
Continues topic across speakers	Mands
Elaborates on own old topic	Calls
Requests information	Imitates others
Makes statements/comments/descriptions	Repeats own utterance
Gives acknowledgments	Repairs
Responds to questions and requests	Captures presupposition/implicature of previous utterance

mentally more advanced forms. Each error-free sentence is given an extra point. Each sentence is then given a score, the scores of all the sentences are summed, and a mean sentence score (DSS) is computed. An expressive language level can be obtained by examining normative findings and matching the subject's DSS to the age level at which 50% of the children achieved a similar score. Norms are based on findings from 2- to 7-year-olds.

A.3   *Other Tests: Conditional Tasks*

The conditional tasks were drawn from Reilly 1982.

Procedure 1: *What if?* Using a variety of pictures as stimuli, the subject is asked different questions to elicit all types of conditional sentences: present, generic, predictive, hypothetical, and counterfactual.

Procedure 2: *Pretend.* This task focuses on the spontaneous production of hypotheticals, following an initial model. The examiner says, "We're going to play a pretending game. First I'll pretend to be something and I'll tell you about it. Then it's your turn to pretend to be something and tell *me* about it. If I were a duck, I would swim in the water." Now the examiner encourages the subject to do one.

Procedure 3: *Lion's face construction.* This task is designed to demonstrate comprehension and production of predictive conditionals. On the table are an outline of a lion's face, small colored paper shapes for putting facial features on the lion and a bowl of food rewards (jelly beans, marshmallows, raisins). The examiner says, "We're going to play a game and give the lion a face. I'll go first and show you how it works: 'If you put the eyes on, I'll give you a marshmallow.'" The subject performs the task and is rewarded. Now it is the subject's turn to make up a sentence. The examiner and subject take turns until the face is completed. (NB: Reilly's task involved puppets. I simplified the task for Laura and did not use puppets.)

Procedure 4: *Lion's face transformation.* Once the face of the lion is complete, the subject is asked questions about the lion (for instance, "What if the lion had been an elephant?") in order to elicit counterfactual conditionals.

Procedure 5: *Bears and pigs.* The goal of this task is (1) to investigate comprehension of counterfactuals and (2) to elicit counterfactual consequents. The examiner reads "The Three Little Pigs" and "The Three Bears" to the subject. Then the examiner shows a picture of a situation with a known result (say, the straw house that is blown down by the wolf) and asks what would happen if some crucial variable were altered ("What if the straw house had been made of bricks?").

Procedure 6: *Imitation.* The subject is asked to repeat two tokens of each conditional type.

Appendix B
Description of Some Nonlinguistic Test Procedures

B.1 Classification Tests

In the classification tests (Inhelder and Piaget 1964; Lovell, Mitchell, and Everett 1962) the subject is given paper cutouts that vary in shape (circles and squares), size (large and small), and color (red and blue). She is asked to sort the cutouts into two piles to test whether she will spontaneously sort along one of the three parameters. She is also asked to sort along one parameter and then to shift to a new parameter.

B.2 Classification/Categorization Tests

In the classification/categorization tests (Curtiss, unpub.) the subject is asked to sort pictures according to a conceptual distinction that is codable in English (such as gender or animacy). Specifically, in each task the subject is given a stack of cards and asked, "Which ones belong together? Which ones are (kind of) the same?" There are four such tasks, which test the semantic classes male/female, human/non-human, animate/inanimate, edible/inedible. In the male/female task, for example, the subject is given a stack of pictures, each with a person on it, to see whether she will spontaneously think to sort on the basis of gender (coded in English by the pronominal system). After each sorting the subject is asked why she sorted in that fashion. If she fails to perform the expected sort, the examiner gives an additional trial, guiding the task by presenting each card one at a time and asking, "Does this belong with the ____ or the ____?" These tasks have been normed on children between 2 and 6 years old (Curtiss and Yamada, unpub.). Normal 3-year-olds are able to spontaneously sort pictures on the basis of gender.

B.3   Class Inclusion Tests

In the class inclusion tests (Inhelder and Piaget 1964; Lovell, Mitchell, and Everett 1962) colored squares (red and blue) are placed before the subject in parallel rows of five. The subject is then asked, "Are there more square ones or more blue ones?" In a modified version, Laura was also shown apples and oranges and asked, "Is there more fruit or more apples?"

B.4   Conservation Tests

B.4.1   Length
The subject is shown two Play-doh worms, one straight and one undulating, and is asked to judge whether they are the same length or whether one is longer (after Lovell, Healy, and Rowland 1962). The same procedure is repeated with two sticks of equal length in various configurations (for instance, forming a T or an acute angle).

B.4.2   Solid Quantity
The subject is shown two equal balls of Play-doh and is asked to judge whether they are the same. Next, one ball is rolled into a hot dog, and the subject is asked whether the remaining ball and the hot dog have the same amount of clay or whether one has more (Elkind 1961). Finally, the hot dog is rolled into a cylinder and then broken into three pieces (Uzgiris 1964), and with each transformation the subject is asked to make "same" or "more" judgments.

B.4.3   Liquid Quantity
The subject is shown two identical tall narrow glasses and one low wide glass (Wallach, Wall, and Anderson 1967). The same amount of liquid is poured into each of the two tall glasses. When the liquid from one tall glass is poured into the low wide glass, the subject is asked to make a "same" or "more" judgment. The liquid is then poured into three small glasses (Beard 1963) and the same question is asked.

B.4.4   Weight
The subject is given two balls of clay to hold, one in each hand. Once the subject agrees that both balls weigh the same, transformations are performed on one of the balls (like those in the solid quantity tasks) and the subject is asked to make "same" or "more" judgments with regard to weight (Elkind 1961).

B.4.5   Number

Two parallel rows of crackers—one row of six cheese-bits crackers and one row of six similarly sized matzoh crackers—are placed in front of the subject. Transformations involving spatial displacement are performed, and the subject is asked to make "same" or "more" judgments (Wohlwill and Lowe 1962).

B.5   Dichotic Listening Test

The stimulus tape for the dichotic listening test (E. Zaidel, unpub.) consists of pairs of syllables from the set [bi] *bee*, [di] *dee*, [gi] *gee*, [pi] *pee*, [ti] *tee*, and [ki] *kee*. These syllables were chosen rather than the usual [ba], [da], [ga] series because they can be more readily illustrated; for example, [bi] can be pictured as "B" or "bee" (the insect). The tape was produced at Haskins Laboratories from natural tokens. The subject listens via headphones first to 30 pairs of training items, in which identical stimuli are transmitted to each ear, and then to two "blocks" of 60 dichotic pairs. The subject's task is to identify the item whose name she hears, by pointing to a six-picture array depicting a bee, a girl named "Dee," a boy named "Gee," a pea, tea, and a key. (The subject is trained to associate the girl's picture with the name "Dee" and the boy's picture with "Gee.")

B.6   Disembedding Tests

B.6.1   Embedded Figures Test

In the Preschool Embedded Figures Test (Coates 1972) the subject must locate a simple figure within larger, more complex figures. This is a modified, simplified version of the Children's Embedded Figures Test (Witkin et al. 1971) for use with preschoolers. The methodology is geared specifically to young children; for example, the subject must find a "teepee" (triangle) in the picture of the butterfly.

B.6.2   Figure-Ground Visual Perception Test

On each item in the Southern California Figure-Ground Perception Test (Ayres 1972) the subject's task is to identify, from an array of six simple objects or designs, which three are contained or "embedded" in a larger complex figure. The first part of the test includes familiar objects and the second part geometric figures.

B.7   Environmental Sounds Recognition Test

In the Environmental Sounds Recognition Test (Van Lancker 1982) a tape of familiar environmental sounds is presented and the subject is to identify the sounds.

B.8   Facial Recognition Test

The Test of Facial Recognition (Benton et al. 1975) consists of the following parts:

1 Matching of identical front-view photographs. On each item the subject is presented with a single front-view photograph of a face and is asked to find the same face in an array of six front-view photographs.

2 Matching of front-view photograph with three-quarter-view photographs. On each item the subject is presented with a front-view photograph of a face and must locate the same face three times in an array of six three-quarter-view photographs.

3 Matching of front-view photographs under different lighting conditions. On each item the subject is presented with a fully lit front-view photograph of a face and must locate the same face three times in an array of six photographs of faces that have been taken under varying lighting conditions.

B.9   Familiar Voices Recognition Test

For the familiar voices recognition test, the voices of people familiar to Laura (her father, her mother, her sister JB, a family friend, and myself) were taped, each saying a sentence that gives no clue to the speaker's identity (for example, "Hi, Laura. How are you? I like you very much"). The task is to identify the speakers.

B.10   Gestalt Perception Tests

B.10.1   Mooney Faces Test

On the Mooney Faces test (Mooney 1957) the subject is presented with a series of black and white pictures in very high contrast with many details obliterated, so that perceiving the faces requires closure. The subject's task is to specify whether each of the 40 items is a boy, girl, man, woman, "old" man, or "old" woman.

B.10.2 Perceptual Integration Test

On the Perceptual Integration Test (Elkind, Koegler, and Go 1964) the subject is given, one at a time, a series of seven line drawings. Each drawing depicts identifiable objects arranged so that they in turn depict a larger object (for instance, various kinds of candy arranged to look like a bicycle, fruits arranged to look like a man). On each item the subject is asked, "What do you see?" Young children up to age 6 tend to focus on either the parts or the whole when labeling the pictures (parts being perceived at an earlier age than wholes). Older children demonstrate part-whole integration (for instance, "It's a man made out of fruit"). Elkind, Koegler, and Go tested 195 children from 4 to 9 years of age and found that 75% of 9-year-olds showed part-whole integration.

B.10.3 Visual Closure Test

On the Visual Closure test of the ITPA (Kirk, McCarthy, and Kirk 1968) the subject must find partially hidden items in a complex line drawing.

B.11 Hierarchical Construction Tasks

The first task (modeled after Greenfield and Schneider 1977 and Greenfield 1978; additional models designed by Curtiss and Yamada) is carried out twice: once with blocks and once with sticks. The subject is shown a series of models of increasing complexity and is asked to build identical structures. The models to be replicated range from simple stacks and rows to complex hierarchical structures. The subject is not allowed to see the constructing of each model but is permitted to look at the model as she builds her own. Norms are available from Greenfield and Schneider 1977, Greenfield 1978, and Vereecken 1961.

In the nesting cups task (Greenfield, Nelson, and Saltzman 1972) the subject is asked to nest a set of different-colored cups of graduated sizes. The task consists of several subtasks. For instance, the subject is asked to "put together" first a five-cup set, then a nine-cup set. Normative data are available for 11- to 36-month-old children from Greenfield, Nelson, and Saltzman's study. Curtiss and Yamada have collected additional normative data from 2- to 5-year-olds.

B.12 Logical Sequencing Task

In the logical sequencing task one set of stimuli (set A) features drawings of simple action sequences (for instance, a shoe being tied, a trip to the store); another (set B) features photographs of simple action sequences (for instance, a man making breakfast). A set of pictures is laid out before the subject in scrambled order and she is asked to "Make a story." Once she has rearranged the pictures, she is encouraged to verbalize the story she has created. Curtiss and Yamada have collected norms from children between the ages of 2 and 5.

B.13   Memory Tests

B.13.1   Auditory Memory Span Test
In the Auditory Memory Span Test (Wepman and Morency 1973) the examiner orally presents sequences of unrelated words and the subject is to repeat them. The sequences increase in length from two to six words. The test is normed on 5- to 8-year-olds. Wepman and Morency claim that memory span does not change markedly after age 8. Curtiss and Yamada have collected additional normative data from 2- to 5-year-olds.

B.13.2   Auditory Sequential Memory Test
In the Auditory Sequential Memory test of the ITPA (Kirk, McCarthy, and Kirk 1968) the examiner orally presents sequences of digits, which the subject is to repeat. Kirk, McCarthy, and Kirk's normative population range from 2 to 11 years of age.

B.13.3   Corsi Blocks Test
The Corsi Blocks test (described in Milner 1971) is similar to the Knox Cubes test but includes nine blocks in a random array on a board.

B.13.4   Knox Cubes Test
The materials for the Knox Cubes test are two unsharpened pencils and four equally spaced linearly arranged wooden blocks glued to a strip of wood. The examiner taps out a series with the eraser end of one pencil and the subject is to tap the correct blocks in the correct sequence with her pencil. Each series ranges from two to seven taps in length. Published norms cover the age range of 4½ to 15½ years. Curtiss, Kempler, and Yamada have collected norms from 2- to 4-year-olds.

B.13.5   Memory for Auditory Nonverbal Stimuli Test
In the Memory for Auditory Nonverbal Stimuli (MANS) test (Curtiss Kempler, and Yamada, unpub.) the subject is trained to associate a familiar tape-recorded sound with a particular photograph. For example, upon hearing a bark, the subject is to point to a photo of a

dog. At no time does the examiner name the sounds or the pictures. The instruction is, "When you hear this"—sound is played on the tape—"you point to this"—examiner points to the appropriate picture. Three different sounds are included on the test: a bark, a phone ring, and running water (pictured by a dog, a phone, and a sink). Once the subject learns the associations, sequences of the sounds are played and the subject must point to the corresponding pictures in the correct order. The sequences range in length from one to eight items.

B.13.6   Memory for Designs Test
In the Memory for Designs test (Graham and Kendall 1960) the subject is presented with a series of 15 pictures consisting of geometric designs. Each design is presented for 5 seconds, then taken away. The subject is to draw the designs from memory.

B.13.7   Memory with Verbal Mediation Task
In the Memory with Verbal Mediation task (after Morris 1975) the subject is shown sets of four cards with simple line drawings—for instance, pen, watch, rose, shoe. As each picture is presented, the examiner labels it aloud. Three types of card sets are shown. In type 1 sets all four words are similar phonemically (rhymed). In type 2 sets the words are unrelated, and in type 3 sets the words are conceptually associated. The cards are shown to the subject, then turned over. She is then shown a duplicate of one of the four cards in the set and is asked to recall the other three members of the set. Because the words associated with type 1 cards are phonemically similar, and those associated with type 3 cards are conceptually similar, these features are assumed to function as mnemonic devices in recalling the facedown cards. Five items of each type are given.

B.13.8   Visual Sequential Memory
In the Visual Sequential Memory test of the ITPA (Kirk, McCarthy, and Kirk 1968) the subject is shown (for 10 seconds) a linear sequence of designs that cannot be verbally coded. She is then asked to reproduce the sequence using small white tiles imprinted with the designs. The sequences range in length from two to eight designs.

B.14   Number Concept Tests

B.14.1   Magic Show
Using extremely small number sets (two or three items), the Magic Show (Gelman 1972a,b, 1980) probes number concepts previously

testable only in older children. Using the words *winner* and *loser* rather than *more* and *same*, Gelman was able to explore, among other things, whether young children see displacement and density as relevant to numerosity. In this task the subject is shown two plates, one with two identical objects on it and one with three. After it is established that the three-object plate is the "winner," a series of items follows in which the subject must identify which plate is the "winner." On certain trials—the "winnerless" trials—the two plates have an equal number of objects. (Between items the plates are hidden behind screens and the sets of objects are manipulated by the examiner.) If the subject succeeds on these items, she is given an additional series of items in which the sets of winnerless sets are spatially displaced (for example, the objects are widely or closely spaced). In each item the subject is asked to judge which plate is the "winner," and in "winnerless" trials she is given additional materials and in asked to "make one the winner."

B.14.2   Counting
In the counting task devised by Gelman and Gallistel (1978) the subject is shown sets of items ranging in number from 1 to 19 and is asked to count the items in each set. Her counting behavior is analyzed to determine whether she has acquired the basic counting principles as outlined by Gelman and Gallistel.

The one-to-one principle: ". . . one and only one numeron must be assigned to each item in the set." (p. 91)

The stable order principle: "Numerons used in counting must be used in the same order in any one count as in any other count." (p. 94)

The cardinal principle: "The final numeron assigned to the last object in the set represents a property of the set—its cardinal number." (p. 98)

B.14.3   Infinity
In the infinity task designed by Gelman (1980) the subject is asked questions regarding the concept of infinity, such as "What is the biggest number you can think of?" and "What happens if you add one to it?"

B.14.4   Number Recognition
In the number recognition task the subject is shown an array of printed numbers and is asked to identify the ones the examiner points to.

B.15   Abduction Tests

B.15.1   Rule/Nonrule Governed Learning Test
In the Rule/Nonrule Governed Learning test (Muma and Muma 1979) the subject is shown 50 cards, each containing two pictures of simple objects. The subject is instructed to "Try to guess the picture I'm thinking of." The rule to be learned is based on either color or size (for instance, the subject must point to only blue items). With each guess the subject is told whether her choice was correct or incorrect.

B.15.2   Simple Rule Acquisition Test
The Simple Rule Acquisition test (inspired by Furth 1966) consists of four subtests with 20 trials each. The subject is presented with two cards, one card containing same figures and one card containing different figures. The subject is instructed to "Try to guess the one I'm thinking of" and is told whether her guess was correct or incorrect.

B.16   Sensorimotor Tests

The Uzgiris-Hunt Ordinal Scales of Psychological Development (Uzgiris and Hunt 1975) provide a means of assessing conceptual development during the sensorimotor stage (0–2 years).

B.16.1   Object Concepts
The subject is asked to (1) find an object that is completely covered with a single screen in two places alternately, (2) find an object that is completely covered under one of three single screens, (3) find an object after successive visible displacements, (4) find an object under three superimposed screens, (5) find an object following one invisible displacement with a single screen, and (6) find an object following one invisible displacement with three screens.

B.16.2   Means-Ends
The subject is asked to (1) let go of an object to reach for another, (2) use a relationship of support to obtain an object, and (3) use a string horizontally to obtain an object.

B.17   Seriation Test

The seriation task (Piaget and Inhelder 1959; Inhelder and Piaget 1964; Lovell, Mitchell, and Everett 1962) consists of three subparts: anticipation or prediction of seriation, active seriation, and insertion. The subject is shown a line drawing of a series of Coke bottles arranged by size to illustrate the concept of being "in order." After the picture is removed from view, the subject is shown eight rods of different colors and lengths in a prescribed random linear configuration and is asked to draw what the sticks would look like if they were "in order," using first colored pencils, then a black pencils. The subject then is asked to order the actual rods. In the insertion task the subject is asked to insert two additional rods in a seriated array. There are norms for all phases of this task from Piaget and Inhelder and from Lovell, Mitchell, and Everett, for children between 4 and 9 years of age.

B.18   Spatial Abilities Tests

B.18.1   Stereognosis
In the Stereognosis test (Laurendeau and Pinard 1970) the subject must reach behind a screen with both hands to palpate a series of familiar objects and geometric shapes (embodying both topological and Euclidean relationships). The subject is asked to identify the item she has felt by naming it out loud or by pointing either to a picture of it or to a duplicate item in an array in front of the screen.

B.18.2   Visual Retention Test
In the Visual Retention Test (Benton 1965) 10 designs are presented one at a time and (depending on the version used) the subject is to draw them from memory, copy the designs, or indicate the design shown by pointing to a multiple-choice card, either immediately or after a delay. Laura was given the copying version.

Appendix C
Conversations with Laura

For transcription notation and references to speakers, see note 1 of chapter 4.

Dialogue 1

J: You seem a little sad today, Laura.

L: It's a little sad they have left. An' I told the head leader they're not sure if (they're) gonna set it for, for eighth, eight, our time which will be as, [pauses abruptly] our time an', the girl arrives where it's one, which is in school right now.

S: What country?

L: She's going to An-mission [Ann Arbor] with um, crocodiles, threw up, or threw (or something . . .) that much that much (. . .) yeah, so you know (I'm) not,

S: Who left?

L: A, JB (some) kids, they're now (. . .) Irvine accent. One is in Eureka another accent, I think, it's very soon that they asked us to fly out. ('e) said, "No, sit down." [č]! It was funny too 'cause they won't let us fly (. . .)

S: 'Til when?

L: Until um, there's time.

Dialogue 2

S: What does it mean, to die?

L: It means that my grandmother an' [mʔ] what's that [hamči]? It's some nursing, or the nursing home, or the [mopɛʔ], [momɛʔ], (. . .) [misɛ], right near my school, old school. (Good) now it's right near m' (Well . . .) my school, (actually 'e) should know that.

S: So, what does it mean to die?

L: Yeah, is it right near Mendocino? It's right near [name of school] in fact. They closed down when my grandmom just left. (It's a) old nursing home, she used to. I can't remember her name, she just died, she dies, a month. An' , an' I can't remember her name. (. . .) I think it was [sik] they put in that nursing home, right near Mendocino.

S: Well, what happens when somebody died?

L: Well, my grandmother died in [mɪnšɪn]. You know that [mɪnšɪn], lock in home (. . .) grandmom got out, 8:30 in the morning, she got out. She got out o' [mɪnšɪn] lodge. Huh! D'you hear she miscaped out 'o [mɪnšɪn] lodge? Huh! (d'you hear) they miscaped out! So did the granmum, the granmum, Mendocino. [sisɚt] (told) the wife, met the husband. He was 82. 82!! 'n threw up. They 'ad [ə] bury 'im. [Chuckle in Laura's voice] He threw up sick. That was a time. Ever had (. . .) in ('is) apartment. I think it was when I had my last fish, my friend or something (. . .) 'n I went an' there was newcomers y'know, all (street they were talking 'bout) them dying. They're new to us (an' we haven't had a) meet. They decided to go away, so they're, they know us. Hey, I know it's our next door neighbors. Our French neighbors flew in! From, one of their kids flew in! That's what *I* heard, this happened (if) they got their inpartment, an' they know us, they knowin' us. Ah! I'm not kiddin' they got an 'partment. They found it they were gonna fly back. Fly back.

Dialogue 3

[Family dinner conversation]

M: [to father] She got to tell the story of the three bears today at school.

F: Who did?

M: Mother found this out. Laura did.

F: Laura told it.

L: Yup, up in Mr. Knight's room.

F: Wow.

M: No, let's hear it.

L: I told a big story and my voice, was kinda low. But it was *not*. It was just in my regular voice. [creakiness] I had to (keep) my voice an' the volume [væljum] down. I said, an' my an' oh, this other guy tells you a joke. [gruffly] "Who ate my porridge?! Did did the mommy, daddy bear ate my porridge? Hey!" Now *that* was the kind of voice that's kind of, what is the voice when you talk really low?

M: It's a deep voice, Laura.

L: You mean there're some other words for it too?

M: Sure, bass voice.

L: Bass? An' what else?

M: Oh. They're really all the ones I think of. I suppose there's a few more though,

L: Like what?

M: I don't think of them right now, Laura.

F: Gruff.

M: Gruff. That's a good one.

L: [in a low voice] See, when you talk like this that means that your voice now goes . . .

F: I think you could say it's a hoarse voice,

L: [In a low voice] You could say it's more of a horse.

F: Now, does that mean that it's a horse talking?

L: No! [Amused] It's me talking. [Chuckles] You know what your voice sound like when you('re) um, when you're sort of sick? Your voice can go hoarse. [Makes voice sound hoarse]

M: Mhm. Quite true.

G: Aren't you going to wait for your mother?

M: Yeah, please do wait Laura, for the rest of us before you begin eating.

L: H-o-o-o-o-w [ha:u]. H-o-o-o-o-w [ha:u]—does your voice go down *low*.

F: Horses talking.

L: [Almost slurred] You know whhyyy [w:a:i] your voice can get hoarse when you get sick?

M: [to F] Anytime you want rice in a dish with hot milk and everything tell me.

F: Oh wow! Wow.

M: Do you want it now?

F: Oh, I'll wait a moment.

L: Do you (know) why [wa:i] your voice gets kind of hoarse when you're sick?

M: Yes, I do.

F: Why.

M: Well, I think you're, there's an infection in your throat (isn't it) an' the throat can't function very well,

F: An' your vocal cords get loosened,

M: Oh, is that so too? I didn't know about that.

F: Like loosening the string on a guitar?

L: Yeah!! It's sounds like your voice, it's not really you talkin', it's kind of, you know, hoarse. (. . .) you know,

F: (What happens) when you loosen a string on a guitar, Laura?

L: It sounds, it sounds, doesn't it sound hoarse, or what? [Chuckles]

M: [to F] Why don't I get the rice now, [name], then I can (. . .)

F: OK, why don't you.

L: Sometimes I get up in the morning my voice sounds hoarse. An' then it goes away, whatever it is, goes away.

Dialogue 4

[Conversation about Thanksgiving and other topics. At the outset Laura is telling me about the phone call she made to her parents]

J: An' who'd you get a hold of when you called?

L: M' dad.

J: Your dad? An' what did you ask 'im.

L: I asked him about Thanksgiving.

J: You asked him about Thanksgiving, an' what did he say?

L: He said he'd be glad to pick me up Wednesday.

J: Oh, they're gonna pick you up on Wednesday?

L: Yeah.

J: Before Thanksgiving, and then you're gonna, um go home, are you gonna go home, or are you gonna go to Eureka straight from the hospital?

L: Go to Eureka straight from the hospital.

J: Oh, wow that's gonna be great! I'm so excited for you!

L: [Squeals] I can't hardly wait! [Hugs me]

J: Great!! I like that hug. An' so what (. . .), have you gone to Eureka for Thanksgiving before?

L: Nope.

J: You've never, You've never been, up there for Thanksgiving, huh?

L: Yeah.

J: Oh, don't your cousins live up there? Who lives in Eureka?
    [Sounds in the hallway]

L: It's lunch!

J: No, it's not lunch yet. I know what I'm gonna do. I'll ask Trish to tell us when it's lunch, OK? And, so you and I can be in here peaceful. Shall we, will you ask Trish to tell us when it's lunchtime? Ask Trish.
    [We leave room. I need to prompt Laura each step of the way to ask Bernie (Trish was busy) to tell us when it's lunch]
    [Later on in the conversation]

J: Do you celebrate um Thanksgiving with your whole family usually? Does everybody come home?

L: Yeah.

J: What happens on Thanksgiving?

L: It's Turkey Day.

J: It's Turkey Day, yayy! I love turkey, it's so tasty. My parents bought a microwave recently.

L: They did!?

J: Yeah! And um, the last time I went to visit them, I took a turkey with me and we baked the turkey in the microwave oven. It was really tasty.

L: Oh. What are you doing Thanksgiving?

J: What am I doing Thanksgiving?

L: Yeah.

J: I guess, um, we're gonna go down and be with my family in Irvine.

L: Oh!! I didn't know that.

J: Yeah we are. My family lives in Irvine.

L: That's where my sister JB lives! [Squeals]

J: Yeah, I know, they must live really close by. And you know what? My two brothers and my sister go to UCI.

L: UCI,

J: Yeah, d'you know where that is?

L: Yeah.

J: That's where JB is, isn't it?

L: Yeah.

J: Yeah, that's where my brothers go and my sister, isn't that something?

L: I didn't know you had one.

J: Yeah, I have uh, two brothers and one sister.

L: I have three kids in (. . .) in my family(s).

Notes

Chapter 1

1. Our research group always chose case names to protect the privacy of the individuals being studied. Thus, Laura has always been known as "Marta." However, after discussing the issue with Laura's mother, I've decided to use Laura's real first name here. In fact, Laura may enjoy knowing there is a book about her. Therefore, with apologies to those who already know her by her case name, henceforth "Marta" will be called Laura. I have maintained the use of initials and/or pseudonyms for family members who appear in the examples.
2. Some have found chronological age and attainment of motor milestones to be better predictors of linguistic capacity (Lenneberg 1967; Lenneberg, Nichols, and Rosenberger 1964).

Chapter 2

1. For transcription notation and references to individuals mentioned in conversations, see note 1 of chapter 4.

Chapter 4

1. Transcription notations:
   - L   Laura
   - J   Jeni Yamada
   - S   Susan Curtiss
   - E   Examiner (either J or S)
   - M   Laura's mother
   - H   Laura's eldest sister
   - JB Laura's second older sister
   - A   Laura's third older sister
   - "Jack" Pseudonym for Laura's father
   - F   Laura's father
   - G   Laura's grandmother
        - (X)   Parentheses around an item within an example indicate that we think this is what was said at this point.

(. . .)   A blank space in parentheses indicates a word or phrase that was unintelligible on the audiotape.

X   The uses of italics highlights an item to illustrate a point being made in the text.

[XX]   Phrases in square brackets give contextual notes or other editorial information.

[X]   International Phonetic Alphabet letters in square brackets are phonetic transcriptions.

[name of X]   This expression replaces the name of a person, school, or city that has been deleted in order to protect the privacy of Laura and her family.

2. Perhaps the conceptual and nonlinguistic demands of the tasks were simply too great for her. For example, she may have been unable to remember the task or to keep her attention fixed on it. I addressed these possibilities by explicitly pointing out each answer choice on each item before allowing Laura to respond or by asking her to repeat the test sentence prior to responding (Shorr and Dale 1984).

Shorr and Dale suggest that part of the problem is the nature of the pointing task itself. In reading a test sentence aloud and asking the subject to consider choices in an array that corresponds to that sentence, the researcher creates a situation quite unlike what goes on in true language comprehension. Usually, upon hearing an utterance listeners simply ascribe some meaning to it, be it correct or incorrect. Pointing tests, on the other hand, may be measuring "reflectivity," the capacity to consider and reflect upon a situation and various alternatives. Reflectivity, undoubtedly necessary in problem solving, is depressed in the mentally retarded.

I dealt with this possibility by giving alternate forms of some tests using small figures rather than pictures. Laura still performed poorly. It seemed clear that her production exceeded her comprehension, accounting in part for the nonsensical quality of many of her utterances.

Chapter 6

1. Two sources of cognitive motivation have been described: intrinsic sources, which cause people to explore and learn from an inherent desire to do so, and extrinsic sources, which cause people to learn for external reasons like material gain, comfort, and safety (Haywood 1971; Odom-Brooks and Arnold 1976). Retarded individuals have been noted to lack intrinsic motivation, failing to show the curiosity and exploratory behavior characteristic of normal children. In this respect Laura's behavior was similar to that of other retarded individuals.

Chapter 8

1. Pinker's (1979) six conditions on a theory of language acquisition are

The Learnability Condition
A theory should account for the fact that languages can be learned.

The Equipotentiality Condition
A theory should posit mechanisms broad enough to account for acquisition of any human language.

The Time Condition
A theory should posit mechanisms allowing the child to acquire language within a reasonable time frame—about three years for "the basic components of language skills."

The Input Condition
A theory should involve mechanisms that require information to the child as input.

The Developmental Condition
A theory should make predictions about intermediate stages that are consonant with empirical findings of child language development.

The Cognitive Condition
A theory should posit mechanisms that are consistent with "what is known about the cognitive faculties of the child" (for instance, perceptual, conceptual, memorial, and attentional capacities).

References

Ames, L. B. 1946. The development of the sense of time in the young child. *J. Genet Psychol*, 68:97–126.

Anderson, J. R. 1975. Computer simulation of a language acquisition system: A first report. In R. Solso (ed.) *Information processing and cognition: The Loyola Symposium*. Washington, D.C.: L. Erlbaum Associates.

Antinucci, F., and D. Parisi. 1973. Early language acquisition: A model and some data. In C. A. Ferguson and D. I. Slobin (eds.) *Studies of child language development*. New York: Holt, Rinehart and Winston.

Ayres, A.J. 1972. *Southern California Sensory Integration Tests: Figure-Ground Perception Test*. Los Angeles: Western Psychological Services.

Baldie, B. J. 1976. The acquisition of the passive voice. *J Child Language*, 3:331–348.

Bates, E. 1976. *Language and context: The acquisition of pragmatics*. New York: Academic Press.

Bates, E. 1979. *The emergence of symbols*. New York: Academic Press.

Bates, E., L. Benigni, I. Bretherton, L. Camaioni, and V. Volterra. 1977. From gesture to the first word: On cognitive and social prerequisites. In M. Lewis and L. Rosenblum (eds.) *Origins of behavior: Communication and language*. New York: Wiley.

Bates, E., and B. MacWhinney. 1979. The functionalist approach to the acquisition of grammar. In E. Ochs and B. Schieffelin (eds.) *Developmental pragmatics*. New York: Academic Press.

Bates, E., and B. MacWhinney. 1982. Functionalist approaches to grammar. In Wanner and Gleitman 1982.

Bayles, K. 1979. Communicative profiles in a geriatric population. Doctoral dissertation, University of Arizona.

Beard, R. M. 1963. The order of concept development studies in two fields. *Educ R*, 15(3):228–237.

Beilin, H. 1975. *Studies in the cognitive basis of language development*. New York: Academic Press.

Beilin, H. 1980. Piaget's theory: Refinement, revision, or rejection? In R. H. Kluwe and H. Spada (eds.) *Developmental models of thinking*. New York: Academic Press.

Beilin, H., and B. Lust. 1975. A study of the development of logical and linguistic connectives. In Beilin 1975.

Bellugi, U., H. Sabo, and J. Vaid. 1988. Spatial deficits in children with Williams Syndrome. In J. Stiles-Davis, U. Bellugi, and M. Kritchevsky (eds.) *Spatial cognition: Brain bases and development*. Hillsdale, N.J.: L. Erlbaum Associates.

Benton, A. L. 1965. *Visual Retention Test,* multiple choice forms. Paris: Centre de Psychologie Appliquée.

Benton, A. L., M. W. Van Allen, K. de S. Hamsher, and H. S. Levin. 1975. Test of Facial Recognition. Department of Neurology, University of Iowa Hospitals, Iowa City.

Bever, T. G. 1970. The cognitive basis for linguistic structures. In J. R. Hayes (ed.) *Cognition and the development of language.* New York: Wiley.

Blank, M., M. Gessner, and A. Esposito. 1978. Language without communication: A case study. *J Child Language,* 6:329–352.

Bloom, L. 1970. *Language development: Form and function in emerging grammars.* Cambridge, Mass.: MIT Press.

Bloom, L. 1973. *One word at a time: The use of single-word utterances before syntax.* Mouton: The Hague.

Bloom, L., and M. Lahey. 1978. *Language development and language disorders.* New York: Wiley.

Bloom, L., K. Lifter, and J. Hafitz. 1980. Semantics of verbs and the development of verb inflection in child language. *Language,* 56:386–412.

Bloom, L., L. Rocissano, and L. Hood. 1976. Adult-child discourse: Developmental interaction between information processing and linguistic knowledge. *Cog Psychol,* 8:521–552.

Bloomfield, L. 1933. *Language.* New York: Henry Holt.

Blount, W. 1968. Language and the more severely retarded. *Am J Ment Defic,* 73:21.

Blumstein, S., and W. E. Cooper. 1974. Hemisphere processing of intonation contours. *Cortex,* 10:146–157.

Bohme, K., and W. J. M. Levelt, 1979. Children's use and awareness of natural and syntactic gender in possessive pronouns. Paper presented at the conference on "Linguistic Awareness and Learning to Read," Victoria, British Columbia, Canada.

Bornstein, M. 1985. On the development of color naming in young children: Data and theory. *Brain and Language,* 26:72–93.

Bowerman, M. 1973a. *Early syntactic development: A cross-linguistic study with special reference to Finnish.* Cambridge: Cambridge University Press.

Bowerman, M. 1973b. Structural relationships in children's utterances: Syntactic or semantic? In T. Moore (ed.) *Cognitive development and the acquisition of language.* New York: Academic Press.

Bowerman, M. 1974. Learning the structure of causative verbs: A study in the relationship of cognitive, semantic, and syntactic development. Stanford University Committee on Linguistics, *Papers and Reports on Child Language Development,* 8:142–178.

Bowerman, M. 1976. Semantic factors in the acquisition of rules for word use and sentence construction. In D. Morehead and A. Morehead (eds.) *Directions in normal and deficient child language.* Baltimore, Md.: University Park Press.

Bowerman, M. 1978. Semantic and syntactic development: A review of what, when, and how in language acquisition. In R. Schiefelbusch (ed.) *Bases of language acquisition.* Baltimore, Md.: University Park Press.

Bowerman, M. 1979. The acquisition of complex sentences. In P. Fletcher and M. Garman (eds.) *Language acquisition.* Cambridge: Cambridge University Press.

Bowerman, M. 1982. Reorganizational processes in lexical and syntactic development. In Wanner and Gleitman 1982.

Brainerd, C. 1978. The stage question in cognitive-developmental theory. *Behav Brain Sci* 1(2):173–213.

Bransford, J., and K. Nitsch. 1978. Coming to understand things we could not previously understand. In J. Kavanaugh and W. Strange (eds.) *Speech and language in the laboratory, school, and clinic.* Cambridge, Mass.: MIT Press.

Brown, R. 1973. *A first language.* Cambridge, Mass.: Harvard University Press.

Brown, R., C. Cazden, and U. Bellugi. 1968. The child's grammar from I to III. In J. Hill (ed.) *Minnesota Symposia on Child Psychology, vol. 2.* Minneapolis, Minn.: University of Minnesota Press.

Bruner, J. S. 1974. From communication to language: A psychological perspective. *Cog,* 3:255–287.

Bruner, J. S. 1975. The ontogenesis of speech acts. *J Child Language,* 2:1–19.

Cambon, J., and H. Sinclair. 1974. Relations between syntax and semantics: Are they 'easy to see'? *Br J Psychol,* 65(1):133–140.

Campbell, R., and R. Wales. 1970. The study of language acquisition. In J. Lyons (ed.) *New horizons in linguistics.* Baltimore, Md.: Penguin Books.

Caramazza, A. 1986. On drawing inferences about the structure of normal cognitive systems for the analysis of patterns of impaired performance: The case for single patient studies. *Brain and Cognition,* 5:41–66.

Carmon, A., and I. Nachshon. 1973. Ear asymmetry in perception of emotional and nonverbal stimuli. *Acta Psychologica,* 37:351–357.

Chomsky, C. 1969. *The acquisition of syntax in children from 5 to 10.* Cambridge, Mass.: MIT Press.

Chomsky, N. 1975. *Reflections on language.* New York: Random House.

Chomsky, N. 1980. *Rules and representations.* New York: Columbia University Press.

Clark, E. V. 1974. Some aspects of the conceptual basis for first language acquisition. In R. L. Schiefelbusch and L. L. Lloyd (eds.) *Language perspectives: Acquisition, retardation, and intervention.* Baltimore, Md.: University Park Press.

Clark, E. V. 1975. Knowledge, context, and strategy in the acquisition of meaning. In D. Dato (ed.) *Developmental psycholinguistics: Theory and applications.* 26th Annual Georgetown University Round Table. Washington, D.C.: Georgetown University Press.

Coates, S. 1972. *The Preschool Embedded Figures Test.* Palo Alto, Calif.: Consulting Psychologists Press, Inc.

Condon, W. S., and L. W. Sander. 1974. Synchrony demonstrated between movements of the neonate and adult speech. *Child Dev,* 45:456–462.

Cook, R. B. 1973. Left-right differences in the perception of dichotically presented musical stimuli. *J Mus Therapy,* 10:59–63.

Cook, W. M. 1931. Ability of children in color discrimination. *Child Dev,* 2:303–320.

Corrigan, R. 1978. Language development as related to stage 6 object permanence development. *J Child Language,* 5:173–190.

Cossu, G., and J. Marshall. 1986. Theoretical implications of the hyperlexia syndrome: Two new Italian cases. *Cortex,* 22:579–589.

Cromer, R. 1968. The development of temporal reference during the acquisition of language. Doctoral dissertation, Harvard University.

Cromer, R. 1970. Children are nice to understand: Surface structure clues for the recovery of a deep structure. *Br J Psychol,* 61:397–408.

Cromer, R. 1972. The learning of surface structure clues to deep structure by a puppet show technique. *Q J Exp Psychol,* 24:66–76.

Cromer, R. 1974a. Receptive language in the mentally retarded: Processes and diagnostic distinctions. In R. L. Schiefelbusch (ed.) *Language perspectives: Acquisition, retardation, and intervention.* Baltimore, Md.: University Park Press.

Cromer, R. 1974b. The development of language and cognition: The cognition hypothesis. In D. Foss (ed.) *New Perspectives in child development*. Baltimore, Md.: Penguin.

Cromer, R. 1974c. Child and adult learning of surface structure clues to deep structure using a picture card technique. *J Psycholinguist Res*, 3:1–14.

Cromer, R. 1975. Are subnormals linguistic adults? In N. O'Connor (ed.) *Language, cognitive deficits and retardation*. London: Butterworth.

Cromer, R. 1976a. The cognitive hypothesis for language acquisition and its implications for child language deficiency. In D. M. Morehead and A. E. Morehead (eds.) *Directions in normal and deficient child language*. Baltimore, Md.: University Park Press.

Cromer, R. 1976b. Developmental strategies for language. In V. Hamilton and M. D. Vernon (eds.) *The development of cognitive processes*. London: Academic Press.

Cromer, R. 1981. Reconceptualizing language acquisition and cognitive development. In R. Schiefelbusch and D. Bricker (eds.) *Early language: Acquisition and intervention*. Baltimore, Md.: University Park Press.

Crystal, D., P. Fletcher, and M. Garman. 1976. *The grammatical analysis of language disability: A procedure for assessment and remediation*. London: Edward Arnold.

Curry, F. 1967. A comparison of left-handed and right-handed subjects in verbal and non-verbal dichotic listening tasks. *Cortex*, 3:343–352.

Curry, F. 1968. A comparison of the performance of a right hemispherectomized subject and twenty-five normals on four dichotic listening tasks. *Cortex*, 4: 144–153.

Curtiss, S. 1977. *Genie: A psycholinguistic study of a modern day "wild child."* New York: Academic Press.

Curtiss, S. 1979. Genie: Language and cognition. *UCLA Working Papers in Cognitive Linguistics*, 1:15–62.

Curtiss, S. 1982. Developmental dissociations of language and cognition. In L. Obler and L. Menn (eds.) *Exceptional language and linguistics*. New York: Academic Press.

Curtiss, S. 1988. Abnormal language acquisition and grammar: Evidence for the modularity of language. In L. Hyman and C. N. Li (eds.) *Language, speech, and mind*. London and New York: Routledge.

Curtiss, S., and J. Yamada. 1981. Selectively intact grammatical development in a retarded child. *UCLA Working Papers in Cognitive Linguistics*, 3:61–91.

Curtiss, S., and J. Yamada. Forthcoming. *The Curtiss-Yamada Comprehensive Language Evaluation (CYCLE)*.

Curtiss, S., J. Yamada, and V. Fromkin. 1979. How independent is language? On the question of formal parallels between grammar and action. *UCLA Working Papers in Cognitive Linguistics*, 1:131–157.

De Renzi, E., and P. Faglioni. 1978. Normative data and screening power of a shortened version of the Token Test. *Cortex*, 14:41–49.

De Renzi, E., and H. Spinnler. 1966. Visual recognition in patients with unilateral cerebral disease. *J Nerv Ment Dis*, 142:515–525.

De Renzi, E., and L. Vignolo. 1962. The Token Test: A sensitive test to detect receptive disturbances in aphasics. *Brain*, 85:665–678.

de Villiers, J. 1980. The process of rule-learning in child speech: A new look. In K. Nelson (ed.) *Children's language, vol. 2*. New York: Gardner Press.

Dimond, S. 1980. *Neuropsychology*. London: Butterworth.

DiSimoni, F. 1978. *Adaptation of De Renzi and Vignolo's Token Test for Children*. Boston: Teaching Resources Corporation.

Dobbs, V. H. 1967. Motivational orientation and programmed instruction achievement gain of educable mentally retarded adolescents. Doctoral dissertation, George Peabody College.

Dore, J. 1974. A pragmatic description of early language development. *J Psycholinguist Res*, 4:423–430.

Dore, J. 1975. Holophrases, speech acts, and language universals. *J Child Language*, 2:21–40.

Dore, J. 1977. "Oh them sheriff": A pragmatic analysis of children's responses to questions. In S. Ervin-Tripp and C. Mitchell-Kernan (eds.) *Child discourse*. New York: Academic Press.

Dunn, L., and L. Dunn. 1981. *Peabody Picture Vocabulary Test–Revised*. Circle Pines, Minn.: American Guidance Service.

Eliot, D., and R. Needleman. 1976. The syndrome of hyperlexia. *Brain and Language*, 3:339–349.

Elkind, D. 1961. Children's discovery of the conservation of mass, weight, and volume: Piaget replication study II. *J Genet Psychol*, 98(2):219–227.

Elkind, D. 1978. Perceptual development in children. In B. Glanville and A. Gilpin (eds.) *Readings in Human Development, 78/79*. Guilford, Conn.: Dushkin Publishing Group, Inc.

Elkind, D., R. Koegler, and E. Go. 1964. Studies in perceptual development: II. Part-whole perception. *Child Dev*, 35:81–90.

Ervin, S. 1964. Imitation and structural change in children's language. In E. Lenneberg (ed.) *New directions in the study of language*. Cambridge: Mass.: MIT Press.

Ervin-Tripp, S. 1977. Wait for me, roller-skate. In S. Ervin-Tripp and C. Mitchell-Kernan (eds.) *Child discourse*. New York: Academic Press.

Ferreiro, E. 1971. *Les relations temporelles dans le langage de l'enfant*. Geneva: Droz.

Ferreiro, E., and H. Sinclair. 1971. Temporal relationships in language. *Int J Psychol*, 6:39–47.

Fischer, K. W. 1978. Structural explanation of developmental change. Commentary to C. J. Brainerd's "The stage question in cognitive-developmental theory." *Behav Brain Sci*, 1(2):186.

Flavell, J. H. 1977. *Cognitive development*. Englewood Cliffs, N.J.: Prentice-Hall.

Flavell, J. H. 1978. Developmental stage: Explanans or explanandum? Commentary to C. Brainerd's "The stage question in cognitive-developmental theory." *Behav Brain Sci*, 1(2):187.

Florey, L. 1971. An approach to play and play development. *Am J Occup Ther*, 25(6):275–280.

Fodor, J. 1983. *The modularity of mind*. Cambridge, Mass.: MIT Press.

Fogelman, K. 1970. *Piagetian tests for the primary school*. New York: Humanities Press, Inc.

Friedman, W. J. 1978. Development of time concepts in children. In H. W. Reese and L. P. Lipsitt (eds.) *Adv Child Dev Behav*, 12:267–298.

Fromkin, V., and E. Klima. 1984. General and specific properties of language. In U. Bellugi and M. Studdert-Kennedy (eds.) *Signed and spoken language: Biological constraints on linguistic form*. Weinheim/Deerfield Beach, Fla./Basel: Verlag Chemie.

Furth, H. G. 1966. *Thinking without language: Psychological implications of deafness*. New York: The Free Press.

Gardner, H. 1976. *The shattered mind*. New York: Vintage Books.

Gardner, H. 1983. *Frames of mind*. New York: Basic Books.

Gardner, H. 1985. *The mind's new science: A history of the cognitive revolution*. New York: Basic Books.

Garnica, O. 1978. Non-verbal concomitants of language input to children. In N. Waterson and C. Snow (eds.) *The development of communication*. New York: Wiley.

Garron, D. 1970. Sex-linked, recessive inheritance of spatial and numerical abilities, and Turner's syndrome. *Psychol Rev*, 77(2):147–152.

Garvey, C. 1974. Interaction structures in social play. Paper presented at the American Psychological Association, New Orleans.

Garvey, C. 1977. *Play*. Cambridge, Mass.: Harvard University Press.

Gelman, R. 1972a. Logical capacity of very young children: Number invariance rules. *Child Dev*, 43:75–90.

Gelman, R. 1972b. The nature of development of early number concepts. In H. Reese (ed.) *Adv Child Dev Behav*, 7. New York: Academic Press.

Gelman, R. 1980. What young children know about numbers. *Educ Psychol*, 15(1): 54–68.

Gelman, R., and C. Gallistel. 1978. *The child's understanding of number*. Cambridge, Mass.: Harvard University Press.

Geschwind, N. 1974. The organization of language and the brain. In R. S. Cohen and M. W. Wartofsky (eds.) *Selected papers on language and the brain*. Dordrecht, Holland: D. Reidel.

Geschwind, N., and A. Galaburda. 1987. *Cerebral lateralization*. Cambridge, Mass.: MIT Press.

Gesell, A. 1940. *The first five years of life: A guide to the study of the preschool child*. New York: Harper and Brothers.

Gesell, A., and C. Amatruda. 1940. The study of the individual child. In Gesell 1940.

Ginsburg, H., and S. Opper. 1969. *Piaget's theory of intellectual development: An introduction*. Englewood Cliffs, N.J.: Prentice-Hall.

Givón, T. 1979. *On understanding grammar*. New York: Academic Press.

Gleason, J. B. 1973. Code-switching in children's language. In T. E. Moore (ed.) *Cognitive development and the acquisition of language*. New York: Academic Press.

Gleason, J. B., and S. Weintraub. 1975. The acquisition of routines in child language. Paper presented at the Stanford Child Language Forum, Stanford, Calif.

Goda, S., and B. Griffith. 1962. The spoken language of adolescent retardates and its relation to intelligence, age, and anxiety. *Child Dev*, 33:489–498.

Goldin-Meadow, S., M. E. P. Seligman, and R. Gelman. 1976. Language in the two-year-old. *Cog*, 4:189–202.

Goodglass, H., and E. Kaplan. 1972. *The assessment of aphasia and related disorders*. Philadelphia: Lea and Febiger.

Goodson, B., and P. Greenfield. 1975. The search for structural principles in children's manipulative play: A parallel with linguistic development. *Child Dev*, 46:736–746.

Gopnik, A., and A. Meltzhoff. 1986. Relations between semantic and cognitive development in the one-word stage: The specificity hypothesis. *Child Dev*, 57:1040–1053.

Gordon, H. 1970. Hemispheric asymmetries in the perception of musical chords. *Cortex*, 6(4):387–398.

Graham, F., and B. Kendall. 1960. *Memory for Designs Test*. Missoula, Mont.: Psychological Test Specialists.

Graham, J., and L. Graham. 1971. Language behavior of the mentally retarded: Syntactic characters. *Am J Ment Defic*, 75:623–629.

Graham, N. C. 1968. Short-term memory and syntactic structure in educationally subnormal children. *Lang & Speech*, 11:209–219.

Greenfield, P. 1978. Structural parallels between language and action in development. In A. Lock (ed.) *Action, symbol, and gesture: The emergence of language.* London: Academic Press.

Greenfield, P., K. Nelson, and F. Saltzman. 1972. The development of rulebound strategies for manipulating seriated cups: A parallel between action and grammar. *Cog Psychol*, 3:291–310.

Greenfield, P., and L. Schneider. 1977. Building a tree structure: The development of hierarchical complexity and interrupted strategies in children's constructive activity. *Dev Psychol*, 13:299–313.

Greenfield, P. M., and J. H. Smith. 1976. *The structure of communication in early language development.* New York: Academic Press.

Grice, H. P. 1975. Logic and conversation. In P. Cole and J. L. Morgan (eds.) *Syntax and semantics 3: Speech acts.* New York: Academic Press.

Grimshaw, J. 1981. Form, function, and the language acquisition device. In C.L. Baker and J.J. McCarthy (eds.). *The logical problem of language acquisition.* Cambridge, Ma.: M.I.T. Press.

Hagen, J. W., R. H. Jongeward, Jr., and R. V. Kail, Jr. 1975. Cognitive perspectives on the development of memory. In H. W. Reese (ed.) *Adv Child Dev Behav*, 10:57–101.

Halford, G. S. 1978. Introduction: The structural approach to cognitive development. In J. A. Keats, K. F. Collis, and G. S. Halford (eds.) *Cognitive development: Research based on a neo-Piagetian approach.* Chichester: Wiley.

Halliday, M. A. K. 1975. *Learning how to mean: Explorations in the development of language.* London: Edward Arnold.

Harris, D. 1963. *Children's drawings as measures of intellectual maturity: A revision and extension of the Goodenough Draw-a-Man Test.* New York: Harcourt, Brace, and World.

Harwood, F. W. 1959. *Quantitative study of the speech of Australian children. Lang & Speech*, 2:236–270.

Haywood, H. C. 1971. Individual differences in motivational orientation: A trait approach. In H. I. Day, D. E. Berlyne, and D. E. Hunt (eds.) *Intrinsic motivation: A new direction in education.* New York: Holt, Rinehart and Winston.

Haywood, H. C., and T. D. Wachs. 1966. Size discrimination learning as a function of motivation-hygiene orientation in adolescents. *J Ed Psychol*, 57:279–286.

Haywood, H. C., and S. J. Weaver. 1967. Differential effects of motivational orientation and incentive conditions on motor performance in institutionalized retardates. *Am J Ment Defic*, 72:459–467.

Heilman, K. M., R. Scholes, and R. T. Watson. 1975. Auditory affective agnosia. *J Neurol Neurosurg Psychiatry*, 38:69–72.

Hill, A. 1975. An investigation of calendar calculating by an idiot savant. *Am J Psychiatry*, 132(5):557–560.

Hill, A. 1978. Savants: Mentally retarded individuals with special skills. In N. Ellis (ed.) *International review of research in mental retardation, vol. 9.* New York: Academic Press.

Hopper, P. J. 1979. Aspect and foregrounding in discourse. In T. Givón (ed.) *Discourse and syntax.* New York: Academic Press.

Hopper, P. J., and S. A. Thompson. 1980. Transitivity in grammar and discourse. *Language*, 56:251–300.

Horgan, D. 1978. The development of the full passive. *J Child Language*, 5:65–80.

Howe, M., and J. Smith. 1988. Calendar calculating in "idiot savants": How do they do it? *Br J Psychol*, 79(3):371–386.

Hurst, L., and D. Mulhall. 1988. Another calendar savant. *Br J Psychiatry*, 152: 274–277.

Huttenlocher, J. 1974. The origins of language comprehension. In R. L. Solso (ed.) *Theories in cognitive psychology: The Loyola Symposium*. Potomac, Md.: L. Erlbaum Associates.

Huttenlocher, P., and J. Huttenlocher. 1973. A study of children with hyperlexia. *Neurology*, 23:1107–1116.

Ingram, D. 1971. Transitivity in child language. *Language*, 47:888–909.

Ingram, D. 1975. If and when transformations are acquired by children. In D. Dato (ed.) *Developmental psycholinguistics: Theory and applications*. 26th Annual Georgetown University Round Table. Washington, D.C.: Georgetown University Press.

Ingram, D. 1978. Sensorimotor intelligence and language development. In A. Lock (ed.) *Action, gesture, and symbol*. London: Academic Press.

Inhelder, B., and J. Piaget. 1958. *The growth of logical thinking from childhood to adolescence*. New York: Basic Books.

Inhelder, B., and J. Piaget. 1964. *The early growth of logic in the child*. London: Routledge and Kegan Paul.

Irigaray, L. 1967. Approche psycholinguistique du langage déments. Thèse de doctorat du 3ᵉ cycle, Université de Paris.

Irwin, J. 1948. A battery of tests of speech and hearing. *Speech Monogr*, 15:133–141.

Jaffe, J., D. N. Stern, and J. C. Perry. 1973. "Conversational" coupling of gaze behavior in prelinguistic human development. *J Psycholinguist Res*, 2:321–329.

Jordan, T. E. 1967. Language and mental retardation. In R. L. Scheifelbusch, R. H. Copeland, and J. O. Smith (eds.) *Language and mental retardation*. New York: Holt.

Karlin, I. W., and M. Strazzulla. 1952. Speech and language problems of mentally deficient children. *J Speech Hear Disord*, 17:286–294.

Karmiloff-Smith, A. 1979. Language development after five. In P. Fletcher and M. Garman (eds.) *Language acquisition*. Cambridge: Cambridge University Press.

Keenan, E. O. 1974. Conversational competence in children. *J Child Language*, 1:163–183.

Keenan, E. O., and B. B. Schieffelin. 1976. Topic as a discourse notion: A study of topic in the conversations of children and adults. In C. Li (ed.) *Subject and topic*. New York: Academic Press.

Keil, F. 1980. Development of the ability to perceive ambiguities: Evidence for the task-specificity of a linguistic skill. *J Psycholinguist Res*, 9(3):219–230.

Kelley, K. 1967. *Early syntactic acquisition*. Report No. P-3719. Santa Monica, Calif.: The RAND Corporation.

Kellogg, R. 1970. *Analyzing children's art*. Palo Alto, Calif.: Mayfield Publishing Co.

Kempler, D. 1977. The function of automatic speech. Honors thesis, University of California at Berkeley.

Kendler, H. H., and T. S. Kendler. 1962. Vertical and horizontal processes in problem-solving. *Psychol Rev*, 69:1–16.

Kessel, F. 1970. The role of syntax in children's comprehension from ages six to twelve. *Monogr Soc Res Child Dev*, 35(6, Serial No. 139).

Kimura, D. 1967. Functional asymmetries of the brain in dichotic listening. *Cortex* 3:163–178.

Kirk, S. A., J. J. McCarthy, and W. D. Kirk. 1968. *The Illinois Test of Psycholinguistic Abilities*. Rev. ed. Urbana, Ill.: University of Illinois Press.

Klatsky, R. 1975. *Human memory: Structures and processes*. San Francisco: W. H. Freeman.

Klein, S. 1976. Automatic inference of semantic deep structure rules in generative semantic grammar. In A. Zampoli (ed.) *Computational and mathematical linguistics: Proceedings of 1973 International Conference on Computational Linguistics, Pisa.* Florence: Olschki.

Knox, S. 1974. A play scale. In M. Reilly (ed.) *Play as exploratory learning: Studies of curiosity behavior.* Beverly Hills, Calif.: Sage Publications.

Krashen, S. 1972. Language and the left hemisphere. *UCLA Working Papers in Phonetics*, 24.

Kreutzer, M., C. Leonard, and J. Flavell. 1975. An interview study of children's knowledge about memory. *Monogr Soc Res Child Dev*, 40(1, Serial No. 159).

Landau, B. and Gleitman, L.R. 1985. *Language and experience*. Cambridge, Mass.: Harvard University Press.

Lansdell, H. 1968. Effect of extent of temporal lobe ablations on two lateralized defects. *Physiol Behav*, 3:271–273.

Laurendeau, M., and A. Pinard. 1970. *The development of the concept of space in the child*. New York: International University Press.

Lee, L. 1974. *Developmental sentence analysis*. Evanston, Ill.: Northwestern University Press.

Lee, L., and S. M. Canter. 1971. Developmental sentence scoring: A clinical procedure for estimating syntactic development in children's spontaneous speech. *J Speech Hear Disord*, 36:315–340.

Lee, L., and R. Koenigsknecht. 1974. *Developmental sentence scoring*. Evanston, Ill.: Northwestern University Press.

Lenneberg, E. H. 1967. *Biological foundations of language*. New York: Wiley.

Lenneberg, E. H., I. A. Nichols, and E. F. Rosenberger. 1964. Primitive stages of language development in monogolism. In *Disorders of Communication. Research Publications, Association for Research in Nervous and Mental Disease*, 42:119–137.

Leonard, L. 1975. On differentiating syntactic and semantic features in emerging grammars: Evidence from empty form usage. *J Psycholinguist Res*, 4(4):357–364.

Lesser, R. 1976. Verbal and non-verbal memory components in the Token Test. *Neuropsychologia*, 14:79–85.

Lieberman, P. 1972. *The speech of primates*. The Hague: Mouton.

Limber, J. 1973. The genesis of complex sentences. In T. E. Moore (ed.) *Cognitive development and the acquisition of language*. New York: Academic Press.

Lovell, K., D. Healy, and A. D. Rowland. 1962. Growth of some geometrical concepts. *Child Dev*, 33(4):751–767.

Lovell, K., B. Mitchell, and I. Everett. 1962. An experimental study of the growth of some logical structures. *Br J Psychol*, 53:175–188.

McIntire, M. 1977. The acquisition of American Sign Language hand configurations. *Sign Lang Stud*, 16:247–266.

Macnamara, J. 1972. Cognitive basis of language learning in infants. *Psychol Rev*, 79:1–14.

Macnamara, J. 1977. From sign to language. In J. Macnamara (ed.) *Language learning and thought*. New York: Academic Press.

MacWhinney, B. 1980. Basic syntactic processes. In S. Kuczaj (ed.) *Language development: Syntax and semantics*. Hillsdale, N.J.: L. Erlbaum Associates.

Mandler, J. M. 1979. Categorical and schematic organization in memory. In C. R. Puff (ed.) *Memory, organization and structure.* New York: Academic Press.

Maratsos, M. P. 1976. *The use of definite and indefinite reference in young children: An experimental study of semantic acquisition.* Cambridge: Cambridge University Press.

Maratsos, M. P. 1979. How to get from words to sentences. In D. Aaronson and R. Reiber (eds.) *Perspectives in psycholinguistics.* Hillsdale, N.J.: L. Erlbaum Associates.

Maratsos, M. P., and M. Chalkley. 1980. The internal language of children's syntax: The ontogenesis and representation of syntactic categories. In K. Nelson (ed.) *Children's language, vol. 2.* New York: Gardner Press.

Marshall, J. 1980. On the biology of language acquisition. In D. Caplan (ed.) *Biological Studies of Mental Processes.* Cambridge: MIT Press.

Masland, M., and L. Case. 1968. Limitation of auditory memory as a factor in delayed language development. *Br J Dis Commun* 3:139–142.

Mason, J. (ed.) 1977. *The family of children.* New York: Grosset and Dunlap.

Mecham, M. 1955. The development and application of procedures for measuring speech improvement in mentally defective children. *Am J Ment Defic,* 60:301–306.

Mein, R., and N. O'Connor. 1960. A study of the oral vocabularies of severely subnormal patients. *J Ment Defic Res,* 4:130–143.

Menyuk, P. 1964. Comparison of grammar of children with functionally deviant and normal speech. *J Speech Hear Res,* 7:109–121.

Miller, G. A. 1956. The magical number seven, plus or minus two: Some limits on our capacity for processing information. *Psychol Rev,* 63:81–97.

Miller, J. F. 1981. *Assessing language production in children: Experimental procedures.* Baltimore, Md.: University Park Press.

Miller, L. 1987. Developmentally delayed musical savant's sensitivity to tonal structure. *Am J Ment Defic,* 91(5):467–471.

Milner, B. 1971. Interhemispheric differences and psychological processes. *Br Med Bull,* 27(3):272–277.

Milner, B., and H. L. Teuber. 1968. Alteration of perception and memory in man: Reflections on methods. In L. Weiskrantz (ed.) *Analysis of behavioral change.* New York: Harper and Row.

Money, J. 1964. Two cytogenic syndromes: Psychologic comparisons. I. Intelligence and specific-factor quotients. *J Psychiatr Res,* 2:223–231.

Money, J., and D. Alexander. 1966. Turner's syndrome: Further demonstrations of the presence of specific cognitional deficiencies. *J Med Genet,* 3:47–48.

Mooney, C. 1957. Age in the development of closure ability in children. *Can J Psychol* 11:219–226.

Morehead, D. M., and A. Morehead. 1974. From signal to sign: A Piagetian view of thought and language during the first two years. In R. L. Schiefelbusch and L. L. Lloyd (eds.) *Language perspectives: Acquisition, retardation, and intervention.* Baltimore, Md.: University Park Press.

Morishima, A., and L. Brown. 1976. An idiot savant case report: A retrospective view. *Mental Retardation,* 14:46–47.

Morris, G. P. 1975. Language and memory in the severely retarded. In N. O'Connor (ed.) *Language, cognitive deficits, and retardation.* London: Butterworth.

Muma, J., and D. Muma. 1979. *Muma Assessment Program.* Natural Child Publishing Co.

Nebes, R. 1971. Superiority of the minor hemisphere in commissurotomized man for the perception of part-whole relations. *Cortex,* 7:333–349.

Neimark, E. D. 1970. Model for a thinking machine: An information processing framework for the study of cognitive development. *Merrill-Palmer Q*, 16:345–368.

Nelson, K. 1974. Concept, word, and sentence: Interrelations in acquisition and development. *Psychol Rev*, 81:267–285.

Newcombe, F. 1969. *Missile wounds of the brain: A study of psychological deficits*. London: Oxford University Press.

Newport, E. L. 1977. Motherese: The speech of mothers to young children. In N. J. Castellan, D. B. Pisoni, and G. R. Potts (eds.) *Cognitive theory, vol. 2*. Hillsdale, N.J.: Erlbaum Associates.

Newport, E. L., H. Gleitman, and L. R. Gleitman. 1977. Mother, I'd rather do it myself: Some effects and non-effects of maternal speech style. In Snow and Ferguson 1977.

Nicolich, L. 1977. Beyond sensorimotor intelligence: Assessment of symbolic maturity through analysis of pretend play. *Merrill-Palmer Q*, 23:89–99.

Oakland, T., and R. Williams. 1971. *Auditory perception: Diagnosis and development for language and reading abilities*. Seattle, Wash.: Special Child Publications, Inc.

Ochs, E., and B. Schieffelin. (eds.) 1979. *Developmental pragmatics*. New York: Academic Press.

O'Connor, N., and B. Hermelin. 1987. Visual memory and motor programmes: Their use by idiot-savant artists and controls. *Br J Psychol*, 78(3):307–323.

O'Connor, N., and B. Hermelin. 1989. The memory structure of autistic idiot-savant mnemonists. *Br J Psychol* 80(1):97–111.

Odom-Brooks, P., and D. J. Arnold. 1976. Cognitive development in mental subnormality. In V. Hamilton and M. Vernon (eds.) *The development of cognitive processes*. London: Academic Press.

Osherson, D. N., and T. Wasow. 1976. Task-specificity and species-specificity in the study of language: a methodological note. *Cog*, 4:203–214.

Parisi, D., and F. Antinucci. 1971. Early language development: A second stage. Paper read at the Colloque sur les problèmes actuels de psycholinguistique, CNRS, December. Paris.

Pawley, A., and F. Syder. 1980. One clause at a time hypothesis. Ms., University of Auckland.

Piaget, J. 1926. *The language and thought of the child*. New York: Harcourt, Brace.

Piaget, J. 1951. *Play, dreams, and imitation in childhood*. New York: Norton.

Piaget, J. 1954. *The construction of reality in the child*. New York: Basic Books.

Piaget, J. 1980. The psychogenesis of knowledge and its epistemological significance. In M. Piatelli-Palmarini (ed.) *Language and learning: The debate between Jean Piaget and Noam Chomsky*. Cambridge, Mass.: Harvard University Press.

Piaget, J., and B. Inhelder. 1959. *La genèse des structures logiques élémentaires*. Neuchâtel: Delachaux and Niestle.

Piaget, J., and B. Inhelder. 1967. *The child's conception of space*. Translation of *La représentation de l'espace chez l'enfant*. New York: Norton.

Piatelli-Palmarini, M. 1980. Introduction. In M. Piatelli-Palmarini (ed.) *Language and learning: The debate between Jean Piaget and Noam Chomsky*. Cambridge, Mass.: Harvard University Press.

Piatelli-Palmarini, M. 1987. Ten years later: More chance, less selectivity. In E. Quagliariello, G. Bernardi, and A. Ullmann (eds.) *From enzyme adaptation to Natural Philosophy: Heritage from Jacques Monod*. Elsevier Science Publishers B. V. (Biomedical Division).

Pinker, S. 1979. Formal models of language learning. *Cog*, 7:217–283.

Pinker, S. 1984. *Language learnability and language development.* Cambridge, Mass.: Harvard University Press.

Pinker, S. 1987. The bootstrapping problem in language acquisition. In B. Mac-Whinney (ed.) *Mechanisms of language acquisition.* Hillsdale, N.J.: Erlbaum.

Pinker, S. 1989. *Learnability and cognition.* Cambridge, Mass.: MIT Press.

Prather, P. A., and J. Bacon. 1986. Developmental differences in part/whole identification. *Child Dev*, 57:549–558.

Pullman, H. W. 1981. The relation of the structure of language to performance in mathematics. *J Psycholinguist Res*, 10(3):327–338.

Raven, J. C. 1951. Coloured Progressive Matrices. Beverly Hills, Calif.: Western Psychological Services.

Reber, A. 1973. On psycho-linguistic paradigms. *J Psycholinguist Res*, 2:289–320.

Rees, N. S. 1978. Pragmatics of language: Applications to normal and disordered language development. In R. L. Schiefelbusch (ed.) *Bases of language intervention.* Baltimore, Md.: University Park Press.

Reilly, J. 1982. Acquisition of conditionals in English. Doctoral dissertation, UCLA.

Rice, M. 1984. Cognitive aspects of communicative development. In R. L. Schiefelbusch and J. Pickar (eds.) *The acquisition of communicative competence.* Baltimore, Md.: University Park Press.

Ricks, D. M., and L. Wing. 1976. Language, communication, and the use of symbols. In L. Wing (ed.) *Early childhood autism.* 2nd ed. London: Pergamon Press.

Roeper, T. 1978. Linguistic universals and the acquisition of gerunds. In H. Goodluck and L. Solan (eds.) *Papers in the structure and development of child language.* (University of Massachusetts Occasional Papers in Linguistics, 4). Amherst, Mass.: University of Massachusetts, Department of Linguistics.

Roeper, T. 1981. In pursuit of a deductive model of language acquistion. In C. L. Baker and J. McCarthy (eds.) *The logical problem of language acquisition.* Cambridge, Mass.: MIT Press.

Roeper, T. 1982. The role of universals in the acquisition of gerunds. In Wanner and Gleitman 1982.

Rosch, E. 1978. Principles of categorization. In E. Rosch and B. Lloyd (eds.) *Cognition and categorization.* Hillsdale, N.J.: L. Erlbaum Associates.

Rosch, E., C. B. Mervis, W. D. Gray, D. M. Johnson, and P. Boyes-Braem. 1976. Basic objects in natural categories. *Cog Psychol*, 8:382–439.

Russo, M., and L. Vignolo. 1967. Visual figure-ground discrimination in patients with unilateral cerebral disease. *Cortex*, 3:113–127.

Sachs, J., and J. Devin. 1973. Young children's knowledge of age-appropriate speech styles. Paper presented at the Linguistic Society of America.

Schiefelbusch, R. 1963. Introduction to language studies of mentally retarded children. *J Speech Hear Disord Monograph Supplement*, 10(3).

Schlanger, B. 1954. Environmental influences on the verbal output of mentally retarded children. *J Speech Hear Disord*, 19:339–443.

Schlesinger, H. S., and K. P. Meadow. 1972. *Sound and sign.* Berkeley, Calif.: University of California Press.

Schlesinger, I. M. 1971. The production of utterances and language acquisition. In D. I. Slobin (ed.) *The ontogenesis of grammar: A theoretical symposium.* New York: Academic Press.

Schlesinger, I. M. 1974. Relational concepts underlying language. In R. L. Scheifelbusch and L. L. Lloyd (eds.) *Language perspectives: Acquisition, retardation, and intervention.* Baltimore, Md.: University Park Press.

Schwartz, E. 1974. Characteristics of speech and language development in the child with myelomeningocele and hydrocephalus. *J Speech Hear Disord*, 39:465–468.

Schwartz, M., O. Marin, and E. Saffran. 1979. Dissociations of language function in dementia: A case study. *Brain and Language*, 7:277–306.

Searle, J. R. 1969. *Speech acts*. London: Cambridge University Press.

Searleman, A. 1977. A review of right hemisphere linguistic capabilities. *Psychol Bull*, 84(3):503–528.

Selfe, L. 1977. *Nadia: A case of extraordinary drawing ability in an autistic child*. London: Academic Press.

Shatz, M. 1982. On mechanisms of language acquisition: Can features of the communicative environment account for development? In Wanner and Gleitman 1982.

Shatz, M., and R. Gelman. 1973. The development of communication skills: Modification in the speech of young children as a function of listener. *Monog Soc Res Child Dev*, 38(5):1–37.

Sherman, J. C. 1983. Acquisition of control in complement sentences: The role of structural and lexical factors. Doctoral dissertation, Cornell University.

Sherman, J. C., and B. Lust. 1986. Syntactic and lexical constraints on the acquisition of control in complement sentences. In B. Lust (ed.) *Studies in the acquisition of anaphora, vol. 1*. Dordrecht, Holland: D. Reidel.

Shields, M. M. 1978. The child as psychologist: Construing the social world. In A. Lock (ed.) *Action, gesture and symbol: The emergence of language*. London: Academic Press.

Shorr, D., and P. Dale. 1984. Reflectivity bias in picture-pointing grammatical comprehension tasks. *J Speech Hear Res* 27(4):549–556.

Shultz, T. R., and J. Robillard. 1980. The development of linguistic humor in children: Incongruity through rule violation. In P. McGhee and A. Chapman (eds.) *Children's humor*. New York: Wiley.

Siegel, L. 1984. A longitudinal study of a hyperlexic child: Hyperlexia as a language disorder. *Neuropsychologia*, 22(5):577–585.

Silberberg, N., and M. Silberberg. 1967. Hyperlexia: Specific word recognition skills in young children. *Exceptional Child*, 34:41–42.

Silberberg, N., and M. Silberberg. 1968. Case histories in hyperlexia. *J School Psychol*, 7:3–7.

Silbert, A., P. Wolff, and J. Lilienthal. 1977. Spatial and temporal processing in patients with Turner's syndrome. *Behav Genet*, 7(1):11–21.

Sinclair, H. 1969. Developmental psycholinguistics. In D. Elkind and J. H. Flavell (eds.) *Studies in cognitive development*. New York: Oxford University Press.

Sinclair, H. 1971. Sensorimotor action patterns as a condition for the acquistion of syntax. In R. Huxley and E. Ingram (eds.) *Language acquisition: Models and methods*. New York: Academic Press.

Sinclair-de Zwart, H. 1973. Language acquisition and cognitive development. In T. E. Moore (ed.) *Cognitive development and the acquisition of language*. New York: Academic Press.

Sinclair, H. 1975a. Language and cognition in subnormals: A Piagetian view. In N. O'Connor (ed.) *Language, cognitive deficits, and retardation*. London: Butterworth.

Sinclair, H. 1975b. The role of cognitive structures in language acquisition. In E. H. Lenneberg and E. Lenneberg (eds.) *Foundations of language development, vol. 1*. New York: Academic Press.

Sinclair, H., and E. Ferreiro. 1970. Compréhension, production, et répétition des phrases à mode passif. *Archives Psychologiques*. 40:1–42.

Slobin, D. I. 1971. Developmental psycholinguistics. In W. O. Dingwall (ed.) *A survey of linguistic science*. College Park, Md.: University of Maryland, Linguistic Program.

Slobin, D. I. 1973. Cognitive prerequisites for the development of grammar. In C. A. Ferguson and D. I. Slobin (eds.) *Studies of child language development*. New York: Holt, Rinehart and Winston.

Slobin, D. I. 1977. Language change in childhood and in history. In J. Macnamara (ed.) *Language learning and thought*. New York: Academic Press.

Slobin, D. I., and C. Welsh. 1973. Elicited imitation as a research tool in developmental psycholinguistics. In C. A. Ferguson and D. I. Slobin (eds.) *Studies of child language development*. New York: Holt, Rinehart and Winston.

Snow, C. E. 1972. Mothers' speech to children learning language. *Child Dev*, 43:549–565.

Snow, C. E. 1977. Mothers' speech research: From input to interaction. In Snow and Ferguson 1977.

Snow, C. E., and C. A. Ferguson. 1977. *Talking to children: Language input and acquisition*. Cambridge: Cambridge University Press.

Snyder, L. 1975. Pragmatics in language disabled children: Their prelinguistic and early verbal performatives and presuppositions. Doctoral dissertation, University of Colorado, Boulder.

Spreen, O. 1965a. Language functions in mental retardation: A review 1. *Am J Ment Defic*, 69(4):482–494.

Spreen, O. 1965b. Language functions in mental retardation. A review 2. *Am J Ment Defic*, 70(3):351–362.

Spelke, E. S. 1982. Perceptual knowledge of objects in infancy. In J. Mehler, M. F. Garrett, and E. C. Walker (eds.) *Perspectives in mental representation*. Hillsdale, N.J.: L. Erlbaum Associates.

Springer, S. P., and G. Deutsch. 1981. *Left brain right brain*. San Francisco: W. H. Freeman.

Stern, D. 1971. A micro-analysis of mother-infant interaction. *J Am A Chil*, 10:501–517.

Sugarman, S. 1979. Product and process in the evaluation of early preschool intelligence. *The Quarterly Newsletter of the Laboratory of Comparative Human Cognition*, 1.

Sugarman, S. 1981. The cognitive basis of classification in very young children: An analysis of object-ordering trends. *Child Dev*, 52:1172–1178.

Sugarman, S. 1982. Developmental change in early representational intelligence: Evidence from spatial classification strategies and related verbal expressions. *Cog Psychol*, 14:410–449.

Swisher, L. P., and E. J. Pinsker. 1971. The language characteristics of hyperverbal hydrocephalic children. *Dev Med Child Neurol*, 13:746–755.

Swisher, L. P., and M. T. Sarno. 1969. Token Test scores of three matched patient groups: Left brain-damaged with aphasia, right brain-damaged without aphasia, non-brain-damaged. *Cortex*, 5:264–273.

Tager-Flusberg, H. 1981. On the nature of linguistic functioning in early infantile autism. *J Autism Dev Disord*, 11(1):45–56.

Takata, N. 1974. Play as a prescription. In M. Reilly (ed.) *Play as exploratory learning: Studies of curiosity behavior*. Beverly Hills, Calif.: Sage Publications.

Tallal, P. 1975. Perceptual and linguistic factors in the language impairment of developmental dysphasics: An experimental investigation with the Token Test. *Cortex*, 11:196–205.

Terman, L. M. 1916. *The measurement of intelligence.* Boston: Houghton.

Teuber, H. L., and S. Weinstein. 1956. Ability to discover hidden figures after cerebral lesions. A.M.A. *Arch Neurol Psychiatry,* 76:369–379.

Tew, B. 1979. The "cocktail party syndrome" in children with hydrocephalus and spina bifida. *Br J Dis Commun,* 14:89–101.

Thal, D., and E. Bates. 1988. Language and gesture in late talkers. *J Speech Hear Res,* 31:115–123.

Thal, D., E. Bates, and U. Bellugi. 1989. Language and cognition in two children with Williams syndrome. *J Speech Hear Res* 32(3):489–500.

Toler, S. A., and N. W. Bankson. 1976. Utilization of an interrogative model to evaluate mothers' use and children's comprehension of question forms. *J Speech Hear Disord,* 41(3):301–314.

Townsend, D., and T. Bever. 1977. *Main and subordinate clauses: A study of figure and ground.* Bloomington, Ind.: Indiana University Linguistics Club.

Tremaine, R. 1975. *Syntax and Piagetian operational thought.* Washington, D.C.: Georgetown University Press.

Tulving, E. 1972. Episodic and semantic memory. In E. Tulving and W. Donaldson (eds.) *Organization in memory.* New York: Academic Press.

Uzgiris, I. 1964. Situational generality of conservation. *Child Dev,* 35(3):831–841.

Uzgiris, I., and J. Hunt. 1975. *Assessment in infancy: Cardinal Scales of Psychological Development.* Chicago: University of Illinois Press.

Van Lancker, D. 1975. Heterogeneity in language and speech: Neurolinguistic studies. *UCLA Working Papers in Phonetics,* 29.

Van Lancker, D. Environmental Sounds Recognition Test.

Van Lancker, D., and D. Kempler. 1987. Comprehension of familiar phrases by left- but not right-hemisphere damaged patients. *Brain and Language,* 32:265–277.

Van Lancker, D., J. Kreiman, and J. Cummings. 1989. Voice perception deficits: Neuroanatomical correlates of phonagnosia. *J Clin Exp Neuropsychol,* 11(5): 665–674.

Vereecken, P. 1961. *Spatial development.* Groningen: J. B. Wolters.

Viscott, D. 1970. A musical idiot savant: A psychodynamic study, and some speculations on the creative process. *Psychiatry,* 33(4):494–515.

Vygotsky, L. 1962. *Thought and language.* Cambridge, Mass.: MIT Press. (Originally published, 1934.)

Waber, D. 1979. Neuropsychological aspects of Turner's syndrome. *Dev Med Child Neurol,* 20:58–70.

Wallach, L., A. J. Wall, and L. Anderson. 1967. Number conservation: The roles of reversibility, addition, subtraction, and misleading perceptual cues. *Child Dev,* 38(2):425–442.

Wanner, E., and L. R. Gleitman. 1982. *Language acquisition: The state of the art.* Cambridge: Cambridge University Press.

Warrington, E. K., and M. James. 1967. Tachistoscopic number estimation in patients with unilateral cerebral lesions. *J Neurol Neurosurg Psychiatry,* 30:468–474.

Warrington, E. K., and L. Weiskrantz. 1973. An analysis of short-term and long-term memory defects in man. In J. Deutsch (ed.) *The physiological basis of memory.* New York: Academic Press.

Watson, J. B. 1925. *Behaviorism.* New York: The People's Institute Publishing Co., Inc.

Wepman, J., and A. Morency. 1973. *Auditory Memory Span Test.* Chicago: Language Research Associates, Inc.

Wexler, K., and P. Culicover. 1980. *Formal principles of language acquisition.* Cambridge, Mass.: MIT Press.

Wexler, K., and H. Hamburger. 1973. On the insufficiency of surface data for the learning of transformational languages. In K. Hintikka, J. Moravcsik, and P. Suppes (eds.) *Approaches to natural languages.* Dordrecht, Holland: D. Reidel.

Whitaker, H. 1976. A case of isolation of the language function. In H. Whitaker and H. Whitaker (eds.) *Studies in neurolinguistics, vol. 2.* New York: Academic Press.

Whitaker, H. A., and O. A. Selnes. 1978. Token Test measures of language comprehension in normal children and aphasic adults. In A. Caramazza and E. B. Zurif (eds.) *Language acquisition and language breakdown.* Baltimore, Md.: Johns Hopkins University Press.

Whitehouse, D., and J. C. Harris. 1984. Hyperlexia in infantile autism. *J Autism Dev Disord*, 14(3):281–289.

Whorf, B. L. 1952. *Collected papers on metalinguistics.* Department of State, Foreign Service Institute, Washington, D.C.

Wing, L. 1975. A study of language impairments in severely retarded children. In N. O'Connor (ed.) *Language, cognitive deficits, and retardation.* London: Butterworth.

Witelson, S. 1977. Early hemisphere specialization and interhemispheric plasticity: An empirical and theoretical review. In S. Segalowitz and F. Gruber (eds.) *Language development and neurological theory.* New York: Academic Press.

Witkin, H., P. Oltman, E. Raskin, and S. Karp. 1971. *Embedded Figures Test.* Palo Alto, Calif.: Consulting Psychologists Press, Inc.

Wolfensberger, W., R. Mein, and N. O'Connor. 1963. A study of the oral vocabularies of severely subnormal patients: III. Core vocabulary, verbosity, and repetitiousness. *J Ment Defic Res*, 7:38–45.

Wohlwill, J. F., and R. C. Lowe. 1962. Experimental analysis of the development of the conservation of number. *Child Dev*, 33(1):153–167.

Yamada, J. 1988. The independence of language: Evidence from a retarded hyperlinguistic individual. In L. Hyman and C. N. Li (eds.) *Language, speech, and mind.* New York: Routledge.

Yamada, J. 1983. The independence of language: A case study. Doctoral dissertation, UCLA.

Yamada, J., and S. Curtiss. 1981. The relationship between language and cognition in a case of Turner's syndrome. *UCLA Working Papers in Cognitive Linguistics*, 3:93–115.

Yourcenar, M. 1961. *The memoirs of Hadrian.* New York: Farrar, Strauss.

Zaidel, E. 1977. Unilateral auditory language comprehension on the Token Test following commissurotomy and hemispherectomy. *Neuropsychologia*, 15:1–18.

Zaidel, D., and R. W. Sperry. 1974. Memory impairment after commissurotomy in man. *Brain*, 97:263–272.

Zukow, P. G., J. Reilly, and P. M. Greenfield. 1979. Making the absent present: Facilitating the transition from sensorimotor to linguistic communication. In K. Nelson (ed.) *Children's language, vol. 2.* New York: Gardner Press.

Index

Visual short-term memory. *See* Memory
Volterra, V. 2, 3, 74, 94

Wachs, T.D. 83
Wales, R. 65
Wall, A.J. 23, 82
Wallach, L. 23, 82
Wanner, E. 118
Warrington, E.K. 99, 104
Wasow, T. 94, 117
Watson, R.T. 104
Weaver, S.J. 83
Weinstein, S. 102
Weintraub, S. 71
Weiskrantz, L. 99
Welsh, C. 21
Wepman, J. 25, 99
Wexler, K. 111
Whitaker, H. 5, 117
Whitaker, H.A. 35
Whitehouse, D. 5
Williams, R. 103
William's syndrome 5, 6, 116
Wing, L. 4, 5
Witelson, S. 97
Wohlwill, J.F. 23
Wolfensberger, W. 4, 44
Wolff, P. 5

Yamada, J. 5, 6, 21, 22, 25, 32, 89, 99,
    110
Yourcenar, M. 95

Zaidel, D. 99, 103
Zaidel, E. 25, 35, 103, 114
Zukow, P.G. 5, 65, 113